NEW YORK PATRIOTS

DOROTHY BLACKMAN

North Country Books • Utica, New York

NEW YORK PATRIOTS

ISBN-10 1-59531-020-7
ISBN-13 978-1-59531-020-0

Illustrations by Martha Gulley
Design by Zach Steffen & Rob Igoe, Jr.

Some of the stories featured in this book originally
appeared in *Mohawk Valley USA* magazine.

North Country Books, Inc.
220 Lafayette Street
Utica, New York 13502
www.northcountrybooks.com

CONTENTS

Acknowledgments..iv

Foreword..v

Symon Schermerhorn's Daring Ride: *1690*..........................1

Major Glen's Magic Keyhole: *1690*.................................7

Ethan Allen's Dawn Surprise: *1775*..............................15

John Glover's Foggy Ride: *1776*.................................23

Nathan Hale's Stirring Words: *1776*.............................29

Nicholas Herkimer's Brave Fight: *1777*..........................37

Daniel Morgan's Turkey Call: *1777*..............................51

Benedict Arnold's Winning Trick: *1777*..........................55

George Clinton's Strong Medicine: *1777*.........................65

Icabod Alden's Fatal Mistake: *1778*.............................71

Adam Helmer's Incredible Run: *1778*.............................77

Anthony Wayne's Midnight March: *1779*...........................87

Timothy Murphy's Blazing Rifle: *1780*...........................93

John Paulding's Lucky Find: *1780*..............................105

John Shell's Tough Stand: *1781*................................111

Bibliography..119

About the Author..122

ACKNOWLEDGMENTS

I would like to thank Dennison Payne and Sherri Vibbard, social studies teachers at Edmeston Central School, for their interest in my historical fiction and in sharing the syllabus each used in their classes. This was helpful in choosing incidents in New York State history which would make good supplementary reading for students. I appreciate the work done by Sheila Orlin, Rob Igoe, Jr., Zach Steffen and other staff members of North Country Books as well as that of illustrator Martha Gulley.

Thanks also should go to fellow four-county librarians who sent books on inter-library loan for my extensive research. I have always been grateful for the support of my family and for the relatives and friends who have encouraged my writing efforts through the years.

FOREWORD

I have always had an interest in historical events and stories set in earlier times, especially the Revolutionary War period. Soon after coming to upstate New York I heard of a scout who had run through our area to warn settlers twenty-six miles away of an Indian attack. This account was noted in James Fenimore Cooper's book, *Drums Along the Mohawk*. I felt it should be written in a version for young readers. Thus I wrote about Adam Helmer and sent it to a magazine I happened to see in a bookstore, *Mohawk Valley USA*. The story was accepted and they asked for others. I continued to research and write stories until there were enough to fill a book.

Some of the stories will be familiar to young readers and others might reveal new information. Readers are invited to ride with Simon Schermerhorn on the snowy road to Albany and storm the fort at Ticonderoga in a surprise attack. Those interested in military strategy could read of General Nicholas Herkimer's courageous direction of the battle of Oriskany. Benedict Arnold is remembered for his treason, but he was a brave fighter for the colonists in earlier days. Here at Watervliet he can be seen using a clever trick to fool the British.

We do not know everything the characters felt or said, but all of these events are as accurate as extensive research could make them. As long as these stories are remembered the efforts of our early patriots live on. At each retelling we repay the debt we owe to them.

Mohawk
River

Schenectady

N

Albany

Hudson
River

-1690-

SYMON SCHERMERHORN'S DARING RIDE

Schenectady, 1690

Symon Schermerhorn and his friend Paul sat at an oak table in the public house in Schenectady. It was the coldest night in this winter of 1690, and they were enjoying a glass of mulled cider before going to their homes.

"B-r-r! I hate to go back out into that freezing night!" Paul said.

"Well, it's the only way we can get into our warm beds," Symon reasoned. "Besides, my dog Bruno will be wanting his supper."

Paul started to reply, but his voice was drowned out by the singing of soldiers coming in the door. They stamped their feet and pressed close to the large fireplace.

Paul leaned across the table and spoke in a low tone.

"Sy, I thought the town leaders sent all the soldiers away."

Symon shrugged. He glanced over his shoulder before answering. "All I know is that we've had nothing but arguments ever since they arrived. Seems Albany got them here from Connecticut to protect us, but the people don't think there's any danger."

"That's what I heard too. I suppose no one would bother with just eighty houses, especially as we're surrounded by a strong stockade."

"I hope not," Symon answered with a worried frown. "Still, we know the French could easily come down from Canada with their Indian fighters."

"For goodness sake, how? They'd be up to their waists in snow the minute they came to the woods. Then when they got to open ground there'd be slush— not to mention the impossibility of crossing the Mohawk."

"But it's been bitter cold today. Maybe the river will freeze and they can walk across," Symon suggested.

Paul burst out laughing, drawing the attention of one of the soldiers who swaggered over to the young men's table.

"Glad to see you people can still find something humorous in this frozen settlement. I for one will be happy to be out of it."

"You're all really leaving, then?" Paul asked boldly.

"No need to stay where we're not welcome. We've been informed that the four hundred inhabitants can take care of themselves. That suits me. Someone else can take that beastly watch at the gates, starting tonight."

Symon stood up and pulled on his coat. "I'm late now, so will see you tomorrow, Paul."

"Yes. I'll just finish and be along soon."

Symon shivered as he stepped out into the cold night. Snow beat against him, stinging his eyes. He saw that the wind had whipped drifts along the fences and buildings. He glanced toward the gate at the south end of the stockade and was surprised to see several soldiers forming a large ball of snow. He went over to them and saw that they were making a snowman! A completed figure stood by the other side of the gate.

"What in the world is going on?" he asked.

"What does it look like?" one soldier replied.

"There's no need for us to spend a useless night guarding against ghost attackers who never come. These men can stand the cold better than we can. We're going to get some sleep," said another.

Symon felt a moment of apprehension but agreed that no army would attempt to move in a blizzard like this. He hurried along to his small house, which was huddled among the larger dwellings. After he fed his dog and did a few chores, Symon went to bed to get warm. The snow was now quite high on his window sill.

He had just fallen asleep when a growl awakened him. "Go to sleep, Bruno," he murmured. But the dog continued to make noises deep in his throat, pacing back and forth between the bed and the window.

Finally Symon gave in and threw back the blankets. "What do you see, Bruno?" he asked with a yawn. He looked out the window and froze in terror.

Shadowy shapes crept in two rows from the unguarded gates to surround the houses. The French! Impossible, but here they were! There was no chance of defending the town now that the army was within the stockade. The only hope was for Symon to try to ride past them and get to the Albany road.

He struggled into his clothes with trembling hands and then threw on his greatcoat. He pushed Bruno into the closet with his food and water. Perhaps he would escape notice there.

Symon crept out of the house and into the barn. The horse was eating when her master softly closed the door behind him and quietly saddled the mare. He carefully eased the horse through the door and jumped onto her back. Then he made a rush for the north gate.

As he galloped past the soldiers he heard bullets whistle by him. He cried out as one smashed into his leg, but kept up his speed.

The snow-packed road seemed endless. Finally, at five o'clock in the morning, he was at the Albany gate, shouting the alarm to the sentry. He used his last burst of energy to pound through the palisade opening, then collapsed. He could barely give the warning before losing consciousness.

Symon came to much later in a warm room and received the thanks of the grateful inhabitants of the Albany stockade. Although heavy losses were found in Schenectady, Symon Schermerhorn had warned Albany in time by his daring winter ride.

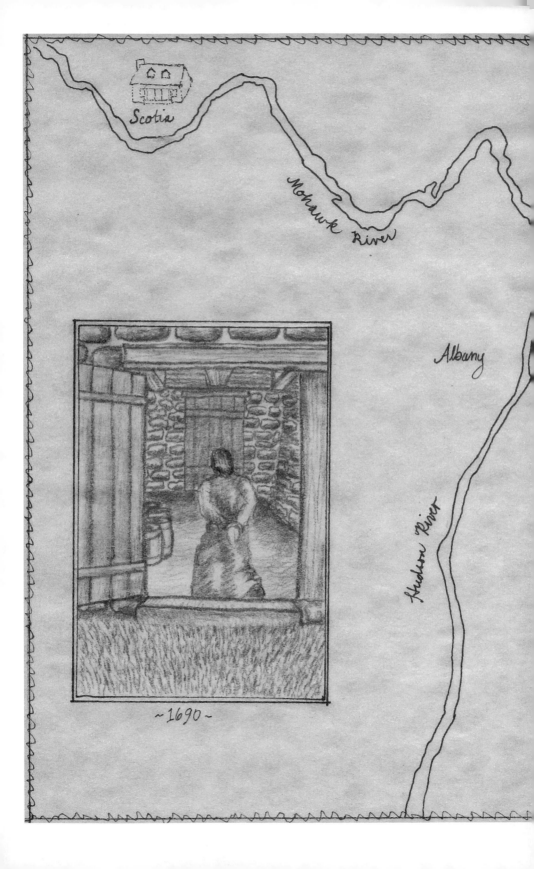

Scotia

Mohawk River

Albany

Hudson River

~ 1690 ~

MAJOR GLEN'S
MAGIC KEYHOLE
Scotia, 1690

One summer evening in 1690, Major John Alexander Glen was riding home to Scotia, New York from a short trip. As the sun went down behind the blue hills, he urged his horse forward. But as he approached his house, he saw something that made his stomach muscles tighten. Two men were walking toward his front door.

The Major never liked to leave his family alone. His wife, Annetje, was very kind-hearted, and his daughters were young and trusting. He feared that they would hesitate to use the weapons he'd left for their protection.

When he arrived at the house, Glen quickly dismounted, relieved to see the men sitting quietly on the porch. As he tied his horse to a post, he saw that one of the men was O-wi-go, a local Indian chief, but he didn't recognize the small white man dressed in a long black gown which was dirty and torn. The family was friendly with the Indians, so he wasn't afraid. However, he was curious about the stranger with the tattered clothes.

Annetje came out to meet him, kissing his cheek in welcome. "I'm so glad you're home at last!" she exclaimed. Then she spoke quietly into his ear. "The Chief has captured this poor French priest."

The Major smiled at his wife. "The dusty trip has made me very thirsty. Please bring us some cold milk, my dear. I'm sure our guests are hungry also." He stepped over to the Chief and extended his hand. "Will you break bread with us, O-wi-go?"

The Indian stood up and greeted his host. As he rose, the Major saw that a leather strap circled the old man's neck, and his hands were loosely bound behind him. He looked completely exhausted.

The Chief nodded. "Food is welcome, friend."

Annetje came out of the house with a pitcher of milk and a large loaf of freshly-baked bread. The delicious smell seemed to revive the priest. He looked gratefully at Annetje and murmured a few words in French. Two of the daughters of the house appeared, carrying platters of meat. As soon as they set these down they rushed back inside.

"The girls are shy," Annetje explained. "Eat hearty," she encouraged them. When she had placed a dish and cup before each one and sliced off slabs of the bread, she also returned to the house.

The Chief untied the prisoner's hands but kept a close watch on him. The three men ate well and in silence. When they'd finished they wiped their mouths with their hands.

Major Glen examined the priest's garment. "O-wi-go, your prisoner's gown is hanging in shreds," he remarked.

The Chief just smiled and went on eating.

"How did you come to capture him?"

The Chief shrugged. "It doesn't matter. Will you keep him for the night? We'll take him tomorrow."

The Major felt sorry for the priest but knew that it was dangerous to oppose the Indians. At least if he were kept in the house he would live for the night. Maybe they could help him somehow.

"I can keep him," he answered. "But what will you do with him tomorrow?" He dreaded to hear the answer.

The chief laughed loudly. "You will see—big fire for Blackrobe!"

Although the priest spoke no English, he trembled when the Indian looked his way. Major Glen realized that the man would be burned at the stake and wished he could prevent this. However, he knew better than to interfere with Indian law.

He simply nodded to show that he understood and started to walk around to the side of the house. The others followed him. Set into the stone wall was a heavy door. He took a key from his pocket and inserted it into the old lock. When the door creaked open, the men peered into a dark cellar room.

The Major stepped inside, and O-wi-go came close behind with the priest. It was very cool in the enclosure, with moisture glistening on the rock walls and the dirt floor damp beneath their feet. The tall Indian had to stoop to avoid hitting his head on the low ceiling. He walked to the back of the room and pushed against another door. It didn't move.

The Major spoke up. "That goes to the kitchen, but

it's barred. We always use this outside door."

The Chief looked everything over—the pans of milk, the salt casks, and the flour kegs. "Good! Blackrobe will stay here," he declared. He removed the strap and the old priest slumped to the floor.

They left the priest huddled against the rough rock wall, and the Major pulled the door shut. He made sure it was tight, then carefully locked it. O-wi-go rattled the door latch. When he was satisfied that his prisoner had no chance of escape, he held out his hand for the key.

The Major handed over the huge brass key. "You have charge of your own prisoner now, O-wi-go. You know he is locked in, and your braves can watch to see that he doesn't break down the kitchen door and go out through the house. I'm too tired to stay awake for very long tonight."

O-wi-go smiled. "Blackrobe is too small and weak to break the door."

After the Chief had left and the young girls of the household were asleep, Major Glen talked with his wife. "Annetje, we must help the poor priest if we can."

"Yes, my husband, but how?"

The Major stepped over to the window and watched the light from the bonfire flicker against the night sky. The drum beats and angry shouts were only a foretaste of what the morning would bring. A shiver ran through his body, and he tried to think of some solution.

"Perhaps the Albany wagon might be an answer..."

"Whatever do you mean, dear?"

"When the neighbor men come by to pick up our

empty casks and kegs..."

"To take them to Albany and bring back full ones. What about it?"

"Well, maybe one of the casks won't be empty!"

Annetje gasped. "You mean to smuggle the priest in a salt cask to Albany? Impossible! He's too big, and he'd surely suffocate."

"We shall see. He is actually quite a small man. And of course he need only stay inside until the wagon is out of the area."

"If the neighbors are willing to take the risk, it might work. At any rate, we must sleep now or we will miss the wagon. They'll take the kegs set outside as usual, won't they?"

"Not if they're not there. We'll bring them inside so the men will have to check with us before they go on."

The couple quietly carried in the kegs which had been standing outside the door. Then they took turns sleeping so they would be sure to catch the wagon.

Just before dawn, the old cart rattled up to the house. One of the neighbors called out for the Major to bring out his casks. Annetje hurried out, holding a finger against her lips, and beckoned them inside. The Major quickly told them his plan and they agreed to help.

They all set to work quietly, although it seemed that the braves on guard were all in a deep sleep. It was difficult to make the priest understand. But he realized that he was going to get away, so he crawled into the cask, shaking and murmuring. The men managed to carry the heavy load up the few cellar steps, through the kitchen and up onto the wagon.

The rescuers were well along the road to Albany when O-wi-go and two braves came down to the cellar door to claim their prisoner. Major Glen was in the barn busy with morning chores, and Annetje and the girls were cleaning up after breakfast when the angry cries began.

The Major came out to see to the problem. Chief O-wi-go slammed the door. When he caught sight of the Major he raged at him. "Where is my prisoner? How could he escape?"

The Major did his best to look amazed. He peeked into the cellar and saw the braves standing there, staring at the walls in puzzlement.

"There certainly was no way to escape using his own strength," he agreed. "You yourself hold the only key. You can see he did not break down the kitchen door, and your men would have seen if he had left through the house."

"Then how did it happen?" the Chief demanded.

Major Glen scratched his head and frowned. Then he snapped his fingers. "I've got the answer! Everyone knows that priests have magic powers. Maybe this one prayed to his Great Spirit. The Great Spirit could have turned the priest into a tiny lizard. He could have crawled out through the keyhole—it must have been magic!"

O-wi-go threw down the key in disgust and stamped away. The braves followed him, looking back with fear until they felt they were far enough away from the magic. And that was the last time a prisoner was brought to the Glen house.

Lake
Champlain

Fort Ticonderoga →

Lake
George

Castleton *

* Skenesboro

N
↑

1775

Hudson River

Mohawk River

Bennington *

ETHAN ALLEN'S DAWN SURPRISE
Ticonderoga, 1775

Bennington, Vermont was peaceful the evening of May 1, 1775, but tension pulsed strongly in the Catamount Tavern. Landlord Stephen Fay was pleased that his taproom was full. It usually was whenever Ethan Allen was there. The Green Mountain boys almost worshiped their rugged leader for his tremendous physical strength and his great courage. The talk was always lively here, especially when their hero let loose with his often profane words. Fay slipped into a corner seat of the dimly lit room, happy to listen quietly. He watched Ethan gulp his cider and rum Stonewall and set the glass down hard.

"I tell you, we must do it, with or without permission. Ticonderoga is the gateway to Canada!"

A young man shifted in his chair. "But Ethan, lots of folks are saying it's best to work for peace."

Ethan slammed a giant fist onto the table. "Best for whom? England? I tell you boys, the tyrants have to be stopped! Every real man has a passion for liberty. The idea electrifies the mind!" He leaned further over the table and lowered his voice. The others moved in closer to hear. "I've sent my brother Heman to the Revolutionary Committee of Correspondence in Connecticut to ask for their help. But if they refuse, we'll cross Lake Champlain on our own. We must capture Fort Ti!"

"Time, Gentlemen," called the landlord. The men raised their glasses in a final toast, "To Liberty!"

Ethan tossed and turned all night, his dreams filled with a possible battle. Then shortly after sunrise he was awakened by the thud of horses' hooves. He threw open the window when he saw his brother dismounting an exhausted horse.

"Heman, do you bring good news?"

"The best. The Hartford authorities want our Green Mountain Boys to take Ticonderoga at once. Colonel Samuel Holden Parsons has three hundred pounds pulled from the colony treasury for this purpose."

"Do you mean that you have the money?"

"No. Bernard Romans and Noah Phelps are coming with it. They'll need some for supplies and to recruit men on the way. They'll be joining us in a day or so."

Ethan's eyes were like bright sparks in his big face. "Let's get the word out—the boys need to leave their plows and fetch their buckskins and guns. We're going on the biggest wolf hunt of our lives!"

As soon as the call was sent out, many backwoodsmen did leave their work, quickly molding bullets and filling powder horns, and marched to Castleton, twenty miles south of the final gathering point, Head's Cove. Ethan, his brothers, and the other leaders made their headquarters at the house of a Richard Bentley. Captain Mott was elected chairman of the war committee. Other members named were Noah Phelps, Epaphras Bull, James Eaton, and John Brown. Ethan was chosen to command the actual assault, with his cousin, Seth Warner, next in command, and James Eaton to follow.

Ethan took immediate charge, calling in Gersham Beach, a blacksmith, to rally all the supporters he could. Then he spoke with Noah Phelps.

"Noah, it is of great importance for us to know the situation at the fort. Try to get inside by pretending to be a farmer looking for a barber. You sure could use a haircut anyway."

The next problem was to obtain boats. Noah Lee, a local fifteen year old, suggested they try the nearby grand estate of the Tory Philip Skene. Thirty men went with Lee to Skenesboro, intending to take Skene's household prisoner as well as find a boat. The war committee also sent a man named Douglas north to Panton to steal more boats.

Ethan was restless all day, anxious for the boats to arrive and worried about his spy at Fort Ti. That evening several of the leaders gathered in the taproom of Zadock Remington's tavern. Noah Phelps burst into the group, pushing past all to reach Ethan.

"Ethan, I did it! I got into the fort and back out without suspicion."

Ethan gave a hearty laugh. "Well done—I see there was indeed a barber on hand!"

Noah ran a hand through his hair and over his

beardless chin. "Yes sir. But the important thing is that the old fort is just waiting to be taken."

"What do you mean? How many troops are there?"

"Only about fifty men! And the walls themselves are crumbling, with a big gap in the south end."

"That's all we need to know!" Ethan roared. "On to Hand's Cove!"

Close to midnight, a quarter-moon shone on the nearly two hundred roughly-dressed men awaiting orders at Hand's Cove. Some carried guns, others had only knives or clubs. Ethan Allen paced the shore, a massive figure in yellow breeches and a green military coat adorned with gold braid. No boats had yet been found, and time was slipping away. The attack must be made by dawn, and it would take two hours to cross Lake Champlain.

Just then Ethan heard scuffling in the distance. A moment later an officer appeared on horseback. He wore the scarlet coat of the Connecticut Governor's Foot Guards. The men grudgingly made way for him, complaining.

"What is this? We don't need company here!" Ethan exclaimed, frowning.

"I am Captain Benedict Arnold, commissioned by the Cambridge Committee of Safety."

"Well?"

"I am in command here."

"Impossible. You are welcome to assist us in the attack, but I, Ethan Allen, am Colonel-Commandant of these troops."

Arnold pulled out papers as proof of his authority, but the militia began pushing, declaring that they would never fight under him. Ethan would command them or they would leave immediately. There were vulgar shouts from the troops—"Hang him! Send him back to Connecticut!"

Ethan again made the offer. "I am the leader of the Green Mountain Boys, with no need of any papers for my authority. However, you may stand beside me as we go, that those who came with you may respect you." Captain Arnold decided then that if the men would go into battle no other way, he had no choice.

Ethan and Seth Warner went again to the point. Here, at last, were two scows. One of the men reported such to Ethan and asked, "How will we get two hundred men across when each boat will only hold fifty? We'll have to make two trips."

Ethan replied, "There will be time for only one trip before dawn. We must go with what we can ferry across."

"Can't we wait until we get more boats?"

"No, surprise is our strongest weapon. If the enemy sees us we are lost. I can capture the fort with just eighty men. Seth, you stay in case more boats do appear."

The troops filled one boat quickly and set forth at once. Stiff north winds made the water choppy, and the overloaded boat nearly took on water, but the men continued to row. As they neared the far shore, the second boat pushed out into the waves.

As the crafts landed at Willow Point, Ethan drew the troops into three ranks. He praised their past efforts and the fact that they had been "a scourge and terror to arbitrary power." "We must this morning quit our pretensions to valor, or possess ourselves of this fortress in a few minutes; and inasmuch as it is a desperate attempt which none but the bravest of men dare undertake, I do not urge it on any contrary to his will." He paused, looking into each face. "You that will undertake voluntarily, poise your firelocks."

At once every man raised his weapon high in the air.

Ethan led the troops quickly and silently along a dirt road, with Colonel Arnold just behind him. They passed a charcoal oven, a redoubt, and an old well before they reached the crumbling outer wall of the fort. Ethan drew his sword and rushed up a short flight of stone stairs which led to the parade ground. A sleepy sentry was at the wicket gate. He frantically pulled the trigger of his musket, but it misfired, flashing in its pan. Panicked, he fled to safety through a covered passageway. The Americans immediately pushed into battle, calling to the astonished British soldiers who straggled forth, "No Quarter! No Quarter!"

Another sentry lashed out, wounding a patriot. Allen struck him in the face with the flat of his sword, knocking the man down. When he begged for mercy, Ethan demanded to see the commander's quarters. The trembling soldier pointed to a stairway.

Ethan bolted up the steps and banged on a door as the Green Mountain Boys filled the area.

"Come out of there, you old rat!" Ethan yelled.

Immediately the door opened. There stood Lieutenant

Jocelyn Feltham, second in command, wearing a coat but clutching his breeches.

"By what authority have you entered His Majesty's fort?" he asked.

Ethan thundered, "In the name of the Great Jehovah and the Continental Congress!"

At this the door of the commandant's room flew open. Colonel William Delaplace stood grim-faced, then handed his sword to Ethan, surrendering his forty men and Fort Ticonderoga. The Americans cheered as the prisoners were paraded through the grounds. The patriots had won the Gate to Canada!

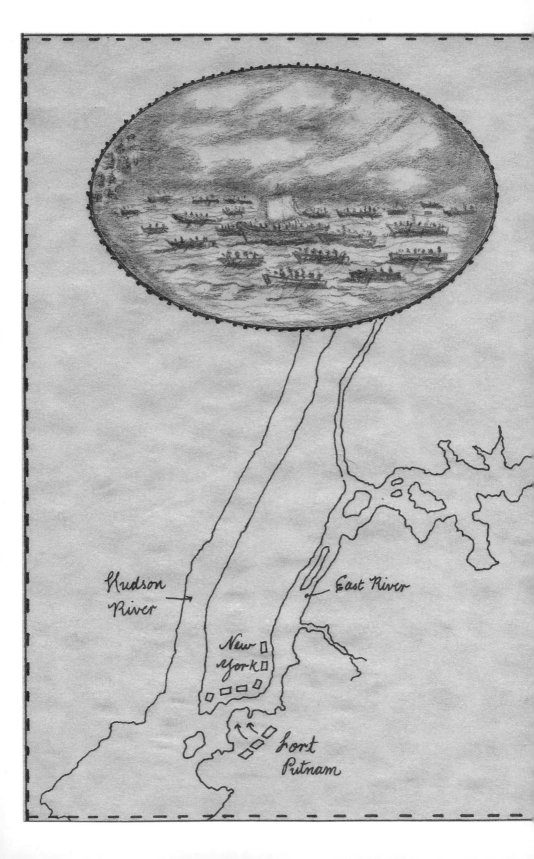

Hudson
River

East River

New
York

Fort
Putnam

JOHN GLOVER'S FOGGY RIDE

Brooklyn Heights, 1776

On an August evening in 1776, rain was slashing down against the grey walls of Fort Putnam on Long Island. A short, red-haired man strode through one of the arches, trailed by a young patriot.

"Well, what news, John? We've all been waiting to hear about your meeting with General Washington."

John Glover turned a handsome profile toward the boy. "There's little time to be wasted in chat, I'm afraid. Our commander-in-chief thinks we've been spared this long from British attack only by a miracle."

"So do we all."

"Well, now he's asking for another miracle and has set General McDougall in charge of it."

"What are you talking about? We're trapped on this tiny strip and can do nothing."

"There is one thing to do and we will do it. We'll ferry the troops across the East River before dawn."

"Impossible!"

"I'd have said so except that Israel Hutchinson and I have been asked to actually work this wondrous feat. I could hardly refuse when the honor of Massachusetts is at stake."

"If it could be done, you two would be the best choice for the task, with your experience in the north shore waters. But it seems overwhelming to think of transporting nearly ten thousand men, not to mention equipment."

"Everything goes—men, baggage, stores—all!"

The boy wiped his forehead. "What about boats?"

"It has been arranged. Now that it is nearly dark they should be arriving. Every small craft in the neighborhood has been collected. The volunteers and militia will come out from the fort first. You must see to the men in your regiment. Absolute silence is a must. We cannot alert the enemy."

Thus, one by one, each regiment was drawn off, leaving a few to see that no chasm showed in the lines. The British were close enough to observe an obvious withdrawal.

John hurried down the path to the ferry landing, passing the marching men with baggage on their backs. He prayed that he could see each one to safety. A hissing sound drew his attention, and he strained to see in the darkness.

"Glover, you old sea dog!"

"Israel! What a piece of work we attempt tonight!"

"Tis nothing for our men from Salem and Marblehead. Surely we've seen worse weather."

"You're correct, as usual, mate. Ho, what's that scuffling there?" John stepped over to a small knot of men fighting to get aboard the first boat.

"If you value your hides, you'd better live up to your reputations and go orderly and silently."

The first oarsmen, tired and hungry, struck out into the threatening water. As they made progress through the waves the northeast wind increased in force. The ebb tide ran so strongly the sloops and other sailboats could not even set forth.

Discouragement was felt in each waiting group. Now there were three challenges for the patriots—time, the tide, and the wind. The boats fought for every foot gained on the mile-wide river. The current was rapid and the rain pelted the forms hunched over the oars.

John held a hand over his eyes for a moment, considering the risks. He took a deep breath before addressing his men. "General Washington is depending on us to save what we can of this operation. We shall do our best, not merely stand here in despair. Next boat, prepare to push off!"

Slowly each small craft launched out into the furious wind. The Marblehead and Salem sailors showed their strength as they strained against the storm. Soldiers shivered on the shore, watching the bobbing rowboats fight the river.

Finally there was no more hope of crossing. Several oarsmen returned, coughing up water, drenched. Angry murmurs ran through the ranks of discouraged men. At the water's edge two older men whispered.

"What is the time now?"

"Nearly eleven o'clock. Our chances for success are

dwindling."

But as the men spoke, the wind suddenly veered dramatically.

"By Jehovah, the wind's shifted to the southwest!"

Men who had been huddled in the fog along the shore, fretting as they waited to go to safety, now jumped into action, quickly filling the remaining vessels and moving out.

Into one of the last boats stepped General Washington. He would always remember how John Glover and the Massachusetts fishermen, against incredible odds, managed to whisk the patriots from under the noses of the British.

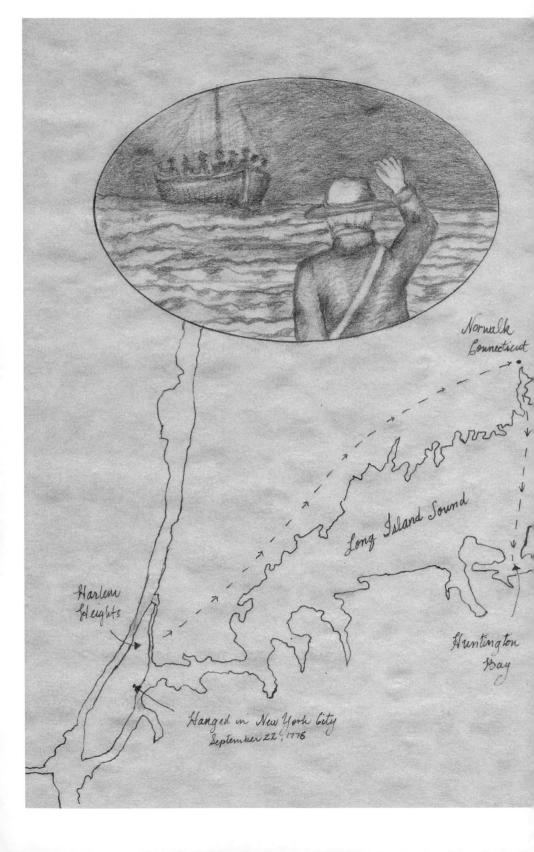

Norwalk
Connecticut

Long Island Sound

Harlem
Heights

Huntington
Bay

Hanged in New York City
September 22, 1776

NATHAN HALE'S
STIRRING WORDS
Harlem Heights, 1776

Lieutenant Colonel Thomas Knowlton paced nervously at his quarters close to New York City. He rubbed his hands together to warm them. September, 1776, was a chilly month. His officers sat before him on hard wooden benches. They knew by the set of his mouth that the news would not be good.

"Men, I am proud that you are called 'Knowlton's Rangers' and proud of all of your scouting work. But the sad truth is that despite all of the danger you have faced, we still lack the information we need about the enemy."

"We know there are enough British guards to keep us too far away to do any good," spoke one man.

"What we really need is someone behind the lines or in the Tory gathering places. Of course he couldn't be in uniform," added another.

"Exactly," the Colonel replied. "I am pleased that you see that a spy is necessary. General Washington himself has requested one from this regiment. I await a volunteer."

A hush fell over the men. Then a muttering began,

growing stronger until one officer spoke out.

"No soldier would want to disgrace himself by skulking about, lying, not even allowed to wear his uniform."

"Of course not," Colonel Knowlton acknowledged, "But yet one must do so for the patriot cause. I shall ask each man individually."

And so he called several by name, each refusing as was his right. No soldier could be compelled to this duty. Shortly he came to Nathan Hale, a tall, sturdy man who had been an athlete at Yale and was a schoolmaster in Connecticut before joining Knowlton's Rangers.

"Nathan Hale, what say you?"

"I will undertake it," the young man replied.

"Thank you, Captain Hale. I know you will serve your country well."

When Nathan returned to his quarters he found his friend William Hull waiting for him.

"Nathan, is it true what they say? You aren't really going to be a spy, are you?"

Nathan laughed. "No one else was keen to go, and I believe I can do it."

"But how could you be disguised? You couldn't wear your uniform."

"No, I think I'll go as a Dutch schoolteacher. At least I know something about that profession."

"But your face will still be uncovered. What about those scars you have from that gunpowder explosion?"

"I'll keep my hat low on my head. Let's see...I'll probably say I'm a Tory looking for a school to teach in. I'll just mix in with the Tories where they socialize."

"Well, I think you've gone mad. However, I'll help you prepare if you are determined to go."

"Thank you, William. You are a good friend. One thing would set my mind at ease. Could you send a message to my family? Tell them that I love them and will be thinking of them."

"Of course. And may God go with you."

Many other rangers spoke to Nathan that night, trying to convince him to change his mind, but he insisted that he would fulfill his duty.

So it was that on September 12, 1776, Nathan left Harlem Heights in search of a safe place to cross Long Island Sound. He had been given a general order to all armed vessels to take him any place he chose. He was accompanied by Sergeant Stephen Hempstead, and the two tried many times to get past the British tenders which rowed close to shore.

Finally, at Norwalk, they reached the American sloop Schuyler. Sergeant Stephen left Nathan on the boat which would take him to Huntington, Long Island.

"Godspeed, Captain Hale. May we meet again."

"I thank you for the escort. Please be good enough to accept these silver shoe buckles. They would not be suitable for a schoolteacher."

Once on board, Nathan changed from his informal uniform to the plain brown cloth suit of a citizen. He made sure that his diploma from Yale was safe, as this would be his proof that he could be a teacher.

Nathan was put ashore in an isolated area of Long Island. It was dawn and no one was around. He hurried to find the closest road and then walked confidently along in his role of schoolteacher. Soon a farmer came by with a load of vegetables. He gave Nathan a ride into town, seeming to accept his story.

Nathan moved boldly about the town, going into several stores, inquiring about work. Then he took a room in a Tory inn. It wasn't long before Nathan learned quite a bit about the number of British troops as he listened carefully to the conversations of the townspeople. Now all he needed was drawings of the British defenses.

One morning Nathan decided to move around the dock area, hoping to pick up even a snippet of news which could help him. He happened upon a farmer and a boatmaster arguing about getting the boat loaded with produce.

"Do you think I'm paying you for my vegetables to sit rotting on the dock?" the angry farmer asked.

"Nothing can be done until the laborers get here to load. I am not a common worker. Let the British wait for their order. I'm sure there is other food in their camp."

Ethan stepped forward. "I would be glad to work at anything. There seems to be no position open at a Tory school so I'd like to try across the river."

The boatmaster scowled at him, then motioned to the piles of bagged vegetables. "Step lively then; everything goes."

The British camp was like a beehive, with workers going in and out and tradesmen scurrying about. Nathan blended in with several groups, estimating the number of troops, the position of the cannons, the amount of ammunition they had, anything he felt might be useful to General Washington. Then he melted into a crowd leaving the camp. He felt lucky that he had been able to finish the task.

Only one thing remained. Nathan quickly engaged a room at an inn. He began to draw pictures of the British defenses on thin paper. He hid this inside of one of his shoes, then went down to the dining area and hastily ate his meal. He paid for his accommodations and went straight to bed so that he could leave early in the morning.

Before dawn broke Nathan slipped out of the inn, heading toward the American lines, which should have been just a few miles away. He moved along the river's edge, hoping to see one of the American patrol boats. It was still quite dark, but he could make out the form of a boat coming near. He signaled, then softly called.

As the boat approached, Nathan realized his mistake. This was a British vessel! As the soldiers brought him aboard, Nathan pretended he was an American deserter. He was taken to the commander-in-chief, General William Howe, as soon as they landed.

General Howe had Nathan searched. He held his breath as the soldiers checked his coat, breeches, shirt and hat. He prayed that they would not lift up the inner sole of his shoe, but the guards were thorough and finally ripped up the soles to find the hidden paper.

"What have you to say for yourself, sir?" General Howe demanded.

"You see for yourself what my orders were. I did what needed to be done for the patriot cause."

"You know what a soldier out of uniform and in disguise is called, don't you?"

"Yes, sir, a spy."

"And were you not aware that the British mete out punishment to spies immediately?"

"I am aware of that, sir."

"I admire your courage, young man, but I must do my duty as well. My order is for you to be hanged tomorrow. You shall have an opportunity to make a last statement, which you may be contemplating."

"I do not have to think about that. I wish to say that I regret that I have but one life to lose for my country."

Nathan Hale was hanged the next morning, ending his service to his country, but his stirring words have inspired patriots throughout the years.

Fort
Stanwix

August 6, 1777

Mohawk

Oriskany

River

Fort Dayton

German
Flatts

NICHOLAS HERKIMER'S
BRAVE FIGHT
Oriskany, 1777

Late one afternoon in July of 1777, General Nicholas Herkimer stepped outside for a breath of air. He leaned against one of the pillars of his spacious brick house and looked over his prosperous farmlands with pleasure. No man enjoyed his home more than he did, but he would have to leave it for awhile. He heaved a sigh as he tamped tobacco into his long clay pipe.

Others across the valley would be relaxing now too, their energies drained by the July heat. But the farmers would work until dusk to use every hour of light. Harvesting their hay and wheat occupied all their thoughts and kept their hands busy. Well, by tomorrow they'd be thinking of other things!

Nicholas dreaded to shatter the peace of the settlements, but the information he'd received would force him to call for every able-bodied man to defend the territory. The British colonel, Barry St. Leger, was approaching with fourteen hundred men, including Iroquois Indians from several tribes.

Worse yet, the wily Mohawk chief, Joseph Brant,

was their leader. Brant was a tough, smart warrior, and Nicholas' own colonels, Cox and Visscher, had told him he should have killed the chief when he'd had the chance.

Nicholas closed his eyes and drew on his pipe. He ran a big hand through his thick gray hair as he thought about the dispatch from Fort Stanwix. The King's forces were to lay siege to the fort and cut communications between it and German Flatts. Nicholas, as commander of the Tryon County Militia, had been asked to send aid. This would not only relieve the fort, but also prevent the conquering of German Flatts. If Fort Dayton fell, the British could advance straight to Albany.

As Nicholas slumped in despair, his young wife appeared with a cold drink. He put his arm around her affectionately.

"Ah, Maria," he said softly in his deep, German-accented voice, "this may be the last glass I sip in peace for a long, long time."

She smoothed the shirt over his round shoulders. "My dear Nicholas," she coaxed, "you look more like a farm worker than the owner. Change your clothes and take me to visit the neighbors."

His dark eyes softened as he looked at her, but he spoke gruffly, "There will be no time for visiting. I must leave for Fort Dayton tomorrow."

They went inside, and in a few minutes he was dictating to his secretary calling his countrymen to war. Nicholas had never learned to write well in English.

Later, when he sat alone, certain phrases from his letter echoed in Nicholas' head. He had called the upcoming battle the "most necessary for the defense of our country" and exhorted "every male person, being in health, from sixteen to sixty years of age…(to) repair immediately with arms."

Those over sixty or in ill health he'd instructed to stay to protect the women and children. Copies of the order would be sent throughout the county. At fifty, Nicholas felt too old to fight and wished to live quietly with his wife in the home he loved. But the men would all fight for their own farms and for their new country.

Within a few days the Tryon Militia, over eight hundred patriots strong, had gathered at Fort Dayton in German Flatts. Nicholas informed them of the battle plan and then gave them some news from Fort Stanwix.

"Men, Colonel Gansevoort has received word that Congress has made a resolution. The United States will have a flag of its own made up of alternating red and white stripes. The union will be represented by thirteen white stars and a blue field. The colonel has had such a flag made up from materials donated by individuals there. It now flies over Fort Stanwix, right in the enemy's face! We must see that it remains there!"

The men cheered and slapped each other's backs, vowing that they'd do the job, all right! Then Nicholas mounted his old white horse and led the soldiers on the beginning of their hard journey. They were a strange looking army, with some uniformed and others not, bringing assorted weapons.

The group traveled all day to cover the ten miles to Stirling Brook, where they made camp. Here an argument developed between Nicholas and some of the officers over which route to take to the fort. But in the morning the small band pressed on, and after another tiring day, settled near Oriskany Creek.

In the evening Nicholas called Adam Helmer, one of the best scouts, to his tent, giving the assignment without delay.

"Adam, word has come from the commander of Fort Stanwix that St. Leger has them surrounded. We must let him know that we're on our way to support him. Take John Damuth and another reliable man with you and get to the fort one way or another. Tell Colonel Gansevoort that we're ready, but he must send out a party of men to create a diversion so we can get through. We can't risk it unless something captures the enemy's attention."

"What about Brant?" Adam asked. "I hear he's in charge of some of the Tories as well as the Indians."

Nicholas sighed. "You know as well as anyone how it will be if we get mixed up with him. We should be able to avoid it by drawing his attention to a division from the fort. You'll probably get to Stanwix by daybreak. As soon as Gansevoort sends out the party, have him fire three cannon shots. That will be our signal to advance."

Adam nodded. "We'll get through all right. But a couple of your colonels won't want to wait for any cannon shots. They're talking of starting out during the night. They show themselves up for the fools they are, thinking this army could get more than one mile in those thick woods by moonlight!"

Nicholas shook the scout's hand. "Pay no attention to them, Adam. They're only talking. They're strong for glory now, but won't be any braver than the rest of us when the action starts. Go along now, and good luck go with you."

Nicholas was wide awake before the next dawn. He was worried about his officers, especially Cox and Visscher. Adam had been right about their restlessness. He'd have to show them who was the leader of this militia! As soon as he'd dressed and breakfasted he sent for all the officers.

When they stood before him, he began. "It won't be long now before we make our march, so keep your men on the alert. As you know, I've sent the messengers ahead to inform Gansevoort of our support. As soon as he's sent out a party, he'll fire three cannon shots. We'll move out then."

Cox frowned, then muttered, "How long will that be?"

Nicholas answered, "They should be at the fort now. The minute the guns sound, we go."

Visscher snorted. "Yeah, after the enemy hears the signal too. I say we should move now!"

Nicholas' dark eyes burned with anger. "I give the orders! It's for you to be sure your men are ready."

Visscher clenched his fists by his sides. "We probably won't even hear the cannon—we'll still be sitting here when St. Leger attacks!"

The officers shifted their feet, eyes darting from Nicholas, to Cox, to Visscher. It grew dangerously silent. Suddenly Cox blurted out, "I know why you wait! You're afraid! Either that, or you're soft on the Tories. Your relatives are in with them, aren't they?"

Nicholas' long upper lip pressed tightly against the lower. A muscle twitched in his cheek. "If we didn't need every fighting man, I'd send you home with the women now!" he replied evenly. "I have nothing to do with my nephew's politics. But if you think that I am afraid ... I ..." He turned away, stiff with anger.

"Let's go, then!" Visscher implored.

The officers' cries rang out, "Yes!" "Yes!" and "We're ready!"

Nicholas spun around and stared at each man in turn. "All right!" he shouted. His flushed cheeks made his eyes seem blacker. "If you must fight, we'll go. But be warned that Brant might set an ambush."

"We're not afraid of Indians!" one officer bragged.

"No, nor all of St. Leger's troops!" another added.

Nicholas mounted his horse and looked down at them. "Just be sure you fight as strongly as you talk when the time comes!" he warned.

"Then we march?" Visscher asked.

"Yes, confound it. March!" Nicholas barked, clamping his teeth down hard onto his pipe stem. He turned his horse away, bitterly aware that he'd been forced into an order against his good judgment. But the officers were so incensed that they might be rash enough to storm ahead anyway. It would be better to lead them than to argue further. At least he might be able to head off trouble.

He'd already urged his horse across the creek before the officers realized their victory. Then they jumped into action, each shouting to his own division. Men scattered in every direction, scrambling to get gear together. Unwashed breakfast pots were banged together and dumped into carts as soldiers called to others down the line to hitch up the oxen. Despite the excitement, they were already listless in the morning heat.

Nicholas muttered behind his grizzled beard as he watched the noisy band form two ragged lines. The fools would wake the dead, to say nothing of alerting the wary Indians.

They'd better settle into proper military order before they meet the British, he thought. Still, he was more worried about what Chief Brant was up to. The Mohawks were quite at home in these woods, and they would guide the Tories.

Before long the humid air had sapped some of the enthusiasm from the troops, and many broke rank to drink from a spring. Others sat by the path whenever they tired.

The scouts plunged ahead, quite heedless of noise. Sometimes the main group pushed along the road ahead of the scouts, who were slowed by underbrush. Nicholas wiped his brow and shook his head. This so-called army would have to be better trained as soon as possible, but he'd need time to turn these eager farmers into tough soldiers. In the meanwhile, they could only do their best. How he wished for rain to clear this oppressive air! And where was that signal? Adam should have been at the fort hours ago! What if they'd all been captured?

Colonel Cox rode up to join Nicholas as he started down the ravine. They descended in silence, as concentration was needed to choose the best path. When they reached the swamp at the foot of the hill, Cox took off his hat and smoothed his hair. Then he returned the cocked brim to its usual angle. He was always conscious of his appearance, even in this withering heat.

Nicholas glanced down at his own worn, blue campaign coat. He was feeling as old as his poor horse. They crossed the log causeway with two companies close behind. Visscher's company would be bringing up the rear, behind the supply wagons. The men had fallen silent, as the heat discouraged idle chatter.

It was extremely quiet here in the dank lowland—too quiet for Nicholas' liking. He felt the hairs along his neck prickle. This was a bad position to be in, and the sooner they got up the other side of the ravine the better he'd feel.

He looked back along the narrow road. It was clogged with soldiers, bunched together, stumbling along. The wagons were coming out of the woods and onto the swamp, their creaking wheels rattling over the last rocks. The scraping of wooden carts against trees sounded unnaturally loud in the stillness.

Nicholas scanned the top of the ravine, eyes narrowed. "I don't like this," he murmured to Cox. "Let's get going!" He urged his horse ahead, starting up the incline. Cox slapped his mount into action and moved past the older white horse.

At that moment, a shot cracked from an unseen rifle, and Cox slipped from his horse, lifeless. Instantly, the swamp and hillside rang with gunfire from both sides, deafening Nicholas. He pressed his horse forward, straining to see the enemy, calling encouragement to his men. Indian war cries filled the air, confirming Nicholas' fear—Brant was behind this ambush, no doubt with much Tory aid.

The enemy fired again and again into the ranks of the militia. Within minutes Nicholas was doubled over with pain on the mossy ground, his horse dead beside him. Then he was lifted and dragged into the brush.

"Careful, careful!" a young voice warned. "It's his knee—support that leg!" Nicholas looked up into the white, frightened faces of his countrymen. He knew they were right to be afraid, but he must not let them see his fear. The pain now tore along his whole leg, and he fought waves of nausea. He knew he must get to a better spot to control the battle before he was completely useless.

He spoke slowly to the soldiers, between stabbing pains, "Help me up to the top of the hill…under that big tree."

The young man looked at him sadly. "I'm sorry, General. You couldn't make it up the incline. You're losing too much blood."

Another spoke then. "It's no use anyway. They'd pick us off for sure. Colonel Visscher has pulled his company back already, and we've lost too many of the rest to stand long."

"What!" Nicholas exploded. "Visscher's bolted? Well, that's just about what I expected of him!" He stared at the others, vainly looking for sign of hope. With man-power so low, the militia would be lucky to get any men out, let alone stop St. Leger's advance.

The air was rank with gunpowder and perspiration. The shooting and screaming hurt Nicholas' pounding head. Then, a few inches from his outstretched hand, a body crashed into a bush. That did it! He had to get his men to higher ground or all would be lost. If he had to crawl up the slope by himself, dragging along by the tree roots, he'd do it!

He started up and rasped out in his deep voice, "I'm still in charge here, and I order you to get me up there immediately! If you disobey, you'll answer for it when we're out of here!" he commanded.

"Yes, Sir, General Herkimer," a soldier replied, snap-ping to life. The others followed, obviously relieved to think that the great man really expected to get them out. It was a tortuous climb and one of them brushed tears from his eyes as he saw his leader bite desperately on his pipe. But at last Nicholas was settled against the trunk of the huge beech tree, grateful for its shade.

Here he could observe the entire field of battle, and he gave orders which were quickly passed along. He tried to study the battle methods of the enemy and fid-geted when the doctor bound up the shattered leg. The patriots were standing their ground, but soon would be suffering. Their ammunition couldn't last long. He noticed that as soon as a soldier fired, an Indian would run up and kill him with a tomahawk, before he could reload his musket.

Nicholas considered this effective strategy. He thought for a minute, then sent the order for the men to start working in pairs. They were to stand behind adjoining trees, but only one man was to fire. He was to shoot and quickly reload while the other stood guard. Then, as an Indian rushed forward with a tomahawk, the partner was to fire. Nicholas was pleased to see this method work time after time.

The air was darkening now and a breeze moved through the leaves, bringing welcome relief. In minutes the younger trees were bending as the wind gained force. Thunder rumbled through the woods, and was followed by a heavy downpour. Lightning flashed across the tree tops, and the fighting died down on both sides. In the sudden bursts of light, Nicholas saw his men lying flat on the hillside, resting. He closed his eyes then and was immediately asleep.

The shower was soon over, and Nicholas awakened to the roar of muskets. He watched the fierce encounter, frustrated not to be there leading his men. But there was an advantage to being right where he was, having an overview and being able to make tactical decisions. He was glad the men had been able to follow his last order, moving to the center of the high ground. They were in a much better position now. If only they could hold out!

The battle continued into its sixth hour, and Nicholas prayed for strength to endure to the end. The militia did seem to be gaining-the furor was subsiding-then, all at once the high wailing of Indians filled the woods. He recognized that cry—"Oonah! O-O-nah!" It grew fainter. Could it be that they...

"General Herkimer! General! They're in retreat—both the Tories and the Indians with them!" The young soldier who had attended Nicholas was laughing and crying at the same time. It was true! The field was left to the militia. Still, St. Leger's forces might come back, and the patriots were terribly weakened. Could they stop the enemy again with their few men?

Nicholas heard it then! Although distant, it was plain to him. Three cannon shots. The messengers had reached Fort Stanwix and the garrison had sent out the diversion. With their main force in retreat with the Indians and the men from the fort taking their attention on the other side, the British would be unable to fight on.

Nicholas turned wearily to the few soldiers nearby. "If only we had the strength to chase them and finish the fight..." he moaned.

"That's not important, General," one replied. "Just think what you've won! With a whole company abandoning us, caught in an ambush, we still beat them off! There was no way to win, but we did! And we did it because of your plans and direction. We kept holding on when we saw your courage."

Nicholas looked around at his brave men, and, for the first time that long day, smiled.

Note: General Herkimer paid the highest price for this victory. He was taken to his beloved home where his leg had to be amputated. The bleeding could not be stopped, and he died from this wound. But he died as he lived, courageously, reading the thirty-eighth psalm aloud to his family.

The Battle of Oriskany was the one most fiercely fought, with the greatest proportion of casualties, but this encounter prevented the advance of British troops and their expected victory in the war.

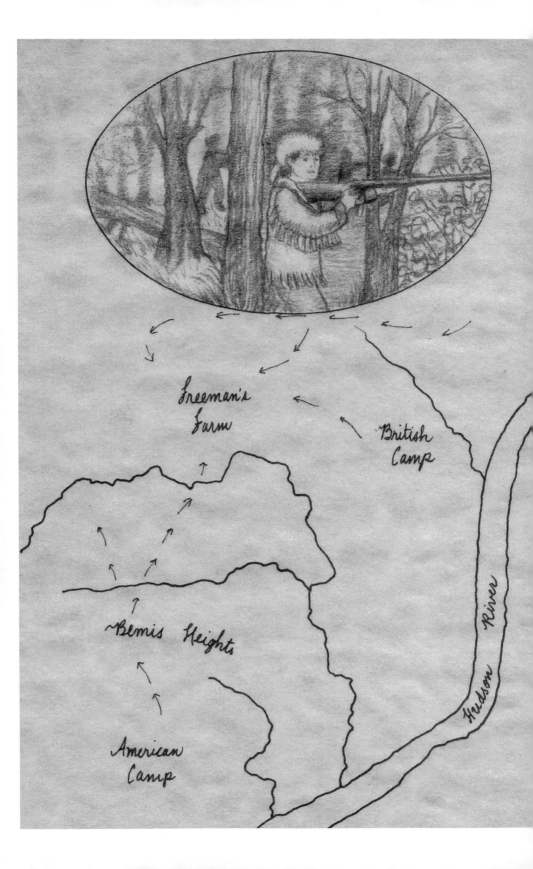

Freeman's Farm

British Camp

Bemis Heights

American Camp

Hudson River

DANIEL MORGAN'S
TURKEY CALL
Saratoga, 1777

September 19, 1777, was a beautiful, crisp but sunny day in Saratoga. "Gentleman Johnny" Burgoyne, a British leader, had been feeling confident about his encampment by Freeman's Farm, a deserted homestead. Then, when several of his soldiers had ventured forth from the area to dig potatoes, they had been shot by an American patrol.

This was the first indication that the American commander Horatio Gates was established on nearby Bemis Heights. Burgoyne decided on a three-pronged attack. He sent General Simon Fraser to go into the fields west of the main farm, and Baron von Reidesel to the Hudson River side, and Burgoyne himself would make the main attack at the center, Freeman's Farm.

Meanwhile, on the Heights, cautious General Gates and impetuous Benedict Arnold argued about the proper procedure. Arnold finally convinced Gates to let Colonel Daniel Morgan's crack rifle corps push forward toward the enemy.

Morgan and his eager men dashed into the woods

and there encountered Fraser's group of Indians and Tories. As usual, surprise and skill quickly stunned the British. However, as the patriots, filled with confidence, rushed across a clearing, they ran right into Burgoyne's main body of soldiers.

The astonished Americans scattered in all directions, leaving Daniel Morgan alone. He was overwhelmed with emotion, at the same time embarrassed, furious, and at the point of tears. How could this humiliation come upon his brave men? Then he took out his special tool to signal his forces to come to him. It was a device used to call turkeys. He sounded the eerie notes of a turkey gobble. The quivering sounds echoed through the trees and slowly all of the rifle corps appeared at Morgan's side. They were ashamed of being routed and doubled their efforts

The men, with their fur caps and fringed shirts, took up positions in the trees. Their long rifles pointed at the British officers and gunners. This time the corps was ready. Burgoyne's companies fired time and again at the camouflaged men, but they had little chance, standing in the open as they did. Soon they were rushing for the shelter of the woods behind them, with Morgan's men in pursuit.

However, the situation was now reversed, with the British in wooded positions and the Americans in open meadows. Daniel Morgan's wild turkey call again sounded, calling the troops back to cover.

Throughout the long afternoon the twenty acre farm changed hands many times. Benedict Arnold fought bravely at this battle, but in the end Baron von Riedesel arrived to support Burgoyne with his German troops. The six-pounders and musketry were too much for the Americans, and they finally left the field and returned to Bemis Heights one mile away.

Technically, the British could claim victory as they held the field, but their losses had all but destroyed them. They had lost many more men than the Americans and were in a most weakened state, both physically and emotionally.

The patriots, now encouraged, handily recaptured nearly all of the positions they'd lost around Ticon-deroga. General Gates' forces still stood between Burgoyne and Albany, thanks to Daniel Morgan's famous turkey call and Benedict Arnold's support.

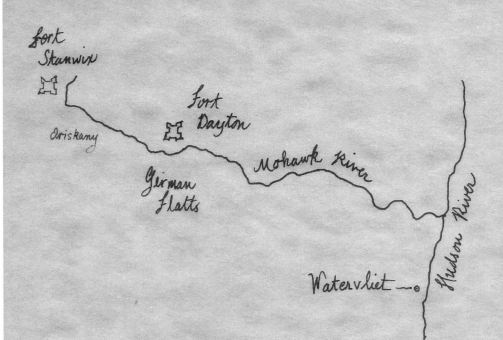

BENEDICT ARNOLD'S WINNING TRICK
Watervliet, 1777

Benedict Arnold paced the floor as he waited for General Schuyler to return to the small room. Their talk had been interrupted when two men on horseback had pounded through the gates looking for the commander. Benedict was here to help General Schuyler in this temporary camp at Watervliet.

General George Washington himself had given him this duty, as he was pleased with Benedict's bravery and skill. His shooting had been very good these past two years, and he hoped to improve in 1777. Now he was receiving at last the appreciation long denied him. Although he had served his country well, the promotions always had gone to others.

Benedict sat down and pulled out the letter he'd received from General Washington last April.

"I am very sensible of the many difficulties you have had to encounter. Your conduct under them does you great credit. As General Thomas will take the burden off your shoulders, I hope you will gather enough strength to finish the important work you have, with so much glory to yourself and service to your country, hitherto conducted."

Suddenly the door swung open and General Schuyler appeared with the two riders, red-eyed and dusty from their journey. He made the introductions quickly. "General Arnold, Colonel Willet and Major Stockwell. They've come from Fort Stanwix to seek aid. The British have it under heavy siege and St. Leger demands immediate surrender."

"I know of Colonel Gansevoort," Benedict said. "He'll never give in."

"Unfortunately, he might not have a choice. The British have seventeen hundred men besides the Tories," Schuyler said.

Major Stockwell spoke then. "We managed to slip away from the fort during the night, and by several hazardous detours, made it to Fort Dayton at German Flatts. We were then able to obtain horses to speed us on our mission."

"Couldn't Herkimer's troops help you hold Stanwix?" Benedict asked. Colonel Willett bowed his head and replied softly, "No, I'm sorry to say that the brave Herkimer died after his leg was amputated. The patriots are in great need of a leader to inspire them to their old strength again."

General Schuyler turned to Benedict. "We all know of your record for fearlessness. Will you command a company of my men and return with these soldiers? There will be no shortage of men willing to march with you. It will merely be a question of the number I can spare."

"You know my answer, of course," Benedict responded. "I was sent to assist you and will do so in the way you decide is best."

"Good!" Schuyler exclaimed. "Our forces, joined with the men at Fort Dayton, will be sure to win the victory and rescue Fort Stanwix!"

By morning there were eight hundred volunteers beginning preparations for the long march. Before the party actually left, General Schuyler received a communication from General Washington which expressed again his confidence in Benedict.

"If the militiamen keep up their spirits, they could, with the reinforcements under General Arnold, be able to raise the siege of Fort Stanwix, which would be a most important matter, just at this time."

Thus encouraged, Benedict started out with enthusiasm. He urged his men to march steadily, and they soon arrived at Fort Dayton. However, they came upon a sorry scene. The Tryon County Militia was in worse shape than reported. Its members were disheartened by the loss of most of their officers. Those not dead or taken prisoner were wounded. The army appeared shattered, and only one hundred patriots responded to Benedict's call to arms. There was nothing to do but delay the march until more soldiers could be found.

The following day, a young man was brought in to Benedict, his hands bound, eyes staring wildly at each wall of the room. The soldiers explained that he was a slow-witted boy who'd been arrested in a recent raid at

Shoemaker's Tavern. He was a spy for the British attending a rally there.

Before they finished speaking, a woman came into the room wailing, followed by a small boy. The scouts tried to push them back, commanding them to leave.

"Go on, get out! There's nothing more to be said—it's over!" The boy sniffled and wiped his face with his sleeve. The woman continued to weep, tearing at her hair and clothes in despair.

Benedict was surprised to have this noisy act in the officers' room—it was more like a gypsy camp! "Why did you bring the prisoner here?" he questioned. "Has he been tried?"

"Yes, and he even admits his guilt," the senior officer answered. "But his mother and brother have disturbed the camp so, we thought we should be sure it was correct to hang anyone guilty, mentally impaired or not. One of the officers had hesitated, but the rest know that is the law."

Another soldier added his opinion, "Yes, he may be slow-thinking but he knows enough to carry tales that could mean death for us all."

At that, the woman ran to Benedict, fell at his feet and clutched his legs. "General Herkimer was my brother!" she exclaimed. "Isn't there any mercy for his relatives?" She sobbed uncontrollably, and then she began to plead for her son's life so passionately that Benedict was touched.

He ran his big hand through his thick black hair and thought hard. It would be too bad to hang an unfortunate boy, but lives might well have been lost…there must be a way… "That's it!" he cried, snapping his fingers.

The woman stopped moaning and stood up. Everyone looked puzzled.

Benedict smiled. "Likes to carry tales, does he? Well, I may have a tale for him to carry if he'd like to bargain for his life. Come here, young man. What is your name?"

The boy stepped forward. "Han Yost Schuyler, Sir."

"Han, you played a dangerous game, spying on your countrymen. Now you must pay the price, which is to hang. But I have thought of a way you might save yourself. Your life could be spared if you were to succeed in carrying a message to St. Leger's troops."

Han wrinkled up his forehead. "Why do you want to talk with your enemy?" he asked.

"I won't be talking to them," Benedict explained patiently. "I want you to take a message about our army. But if you fail, you'll be returned to hang, as your sentence demands."

"Wha…what do I say?" the boy stammered.

"Now listen carefully," Benedict instructed. "Tell them that Benedict Arnold is approaching rapidly with a great army."

"But you don't have a great…"

"Never mind what I have. You just take that message and be sure you convince them that it is true. You can say that you escaped and came to warn them. They'll think you're still loyal to them."

"What if they ask me how many men you have?"

Han persisted.

"Then you can point up to the trees and tell them that I have as many men as there are leaves on the trees!"

"I will. I'll do it, sir."

"To be sure that you do, we'll keep a hostage until I hear that you have carried out my instructions."

The mother burst out, "I'll stay! I know that Han will do just as he says."

Benedict shook his head. "No, my lady, we will not hold a woman hostage. Your other son will stay. I'm sure he is brave enough and trusts his brother. I believe that Han will want to earn a good report so that his young brother can be free."

"Yes. The report will be good," Han declared. "If you'll untie my hands, I'll go now." The soldiers freed him and he started to leave.

"Just a minute," Benedict called, beckoning the boy back. "Take off your coat."

"My coat? What for?"

"You'll see in a minute. Men, take this garment out and shoot several holes in it."

"That's my good coat!" Han protested.

"It may save your life by its tatters," Benedict said. "It should convince the British that you barely escaped with your hide."

They all left but one scout. "That's a smart idea, General Arnold," he said.

"Let's just hope the trick works. Now all we need is another actor to complete the play. Send one of the trusted Oneidas to me."

When an Indian arrived, Benedict explained the plan. This man was to take the same message to the troops, but was to make a large circle and approach from another direction. He was given authority to include one or two other Indians if he thought it advisable.

Later, the officers asked how he thought of the idea.

"Well," Benedict answered, "you saw how defeated the militia was after Oriskany. Believe me, the Indians fared worse. They were forced to retreat, and they're not used to that. They were only supposed to be watching at that battle, but ended up in the fiercest fighting. I'm sure they're close to boiling over with resentment already. I don't think they'll want to risk facing a huge army now."

"We don't have one for them to worry about," the officer said.

"That's not what they'll hear. If they believe the messengers, we'll win. As we don't have the strength, we must have the wit."

Benedict ordered the men to march on, hoping they wouldn't be pitted against terrible odds. But they saw no one on the way. In the distance they were surprised to see scouts from Fort Stanwix gathering equipment apparently left behind by the departing British.

As soon as they neared the gates, Gansevoort himself rushed out to thank Benedict for saving the fort. He told of their shock when the enemy stopped in the midst of heavy firing and just seemed to melt away into the woods.

"We thought it was a trick," Gansevoort said, "so we didn't pursue. Then we sent a few men out to bring in the tents and material left behind in their haste. At night, the boy you sent slipped away from the fleeing British and came to the fort to explain. He is anxious about his brother."

"Well," Benedict said, "he completed his mission— send notification to release his brother."

Everyone crowded around to praise Benedict for his good plan.

"It was just a little trick," Benedict admitted.

Commander Gansevoort nodded. "It was a winning trick, Benedict," he corrected. And all the men shouted their agreement.

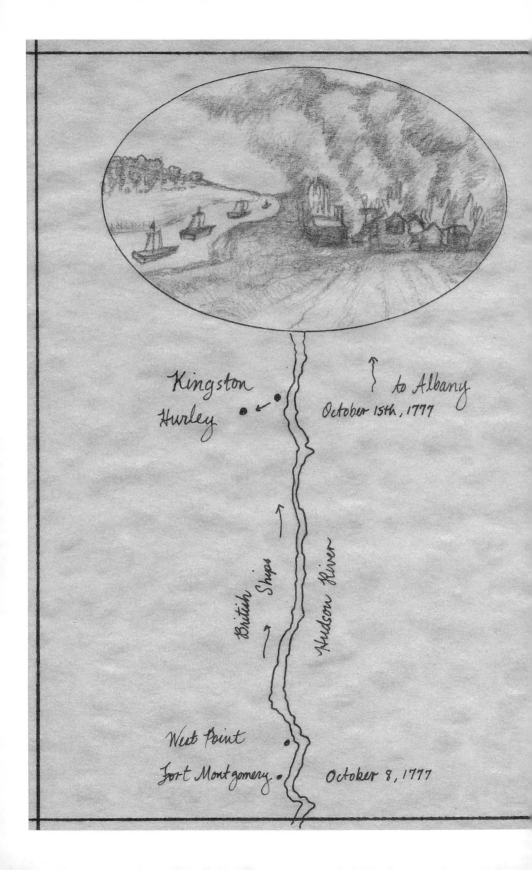

Kingston

Hurley

to Albany

October 15th, 1777

British Ships

Hudson River

West Point

Fort Montgomery

October 8, 1777

GEORGE CLINTON'S STRONG MEDICINE

West Point, 1777

Governor George Clinton leaned against the grey stone wall of Fort Montgomery. For a moment he turned his aching forehead into the welcome coolness. Only three months had passed since he had been inaugurated as the first governor of New York State, but it seemed as if years had gone by. Much had happened since that glad day, very little of it good. He was weary of this command and certainly sick to death of the British. But as one of his fellow officers approached, Clinton drew himself up to his usual military posture. He frowned at the young man's serious expression.

"Well, what say you? Bad news?"

"Sir, troops have been spotted down river."

"How close?"

"Twelve miles, sir. Request permission to send a division to engage them."

"We cannot spare that amount of men. Too many were needed to turn back Burgoyne."

"Surely there still are enough of us to defend the fort against foot soldiers!"

"Of course. Prepare as usual."

Before either man could move, warships came sailing into view. Clinton clenched his fists in the pockets of his coat and ordered full defense.

The battle began soon enough. Although the garrison fought fiercely, the one thousand men were no match for the combined attack from both water and land. Clinton summoned his leaders.

"We cannot win, but we will not surrender. Let each man do the best he can for himself. Make for Kingston. I'll follow and will meet you along the way, please God."

As soon as the order was passed down, men began to slip out of the structure, slowly at first, then in more desperate rushes as the furor of battle increased. At last Clinton took his own sad farewell of Fort Montgomery. He barely escaped, pushing through brush and stumbling over stone until he was able to slide down a steep embankment to the river's edge. He searched until he found a boat which had been well hidden in the growth by the shore. He sat until he could regain his strength, then pushed the boat into the water with great care. He made his silent way north toward Kingston.

Before long Clinton had joined his troops from the garrison. The men were very relieved to have their commander with them again. While the officers were planning their next moves, sentries pressed into the circle, pushing a British prisoner ahead of them.

"Well, what have we here then?" asked Clinton.

"A wretched British spy, sir. Claims to be a Daniel Taylor. Won't say more."

"Oh, won't he? Well, we'll see. Escort him over to that grove of trees. I believe our guest will be anxious to speak soon enough."

As the men moved the prisoner along he began to cough, then pulled one arm free to cover his mouth. Governor Clinton spoke up immediately. "Stop! Go no further. Fetch the strongest medicine we possess."

"What's wrong?" one sentry asked.

"Didn't you see? That coughing was only an excuse and an old one at that. It was to cover up a swallowing of something."

"What, a poison pill?"

"Possibly. But whatever went down will come right back up, and I intend to know what it was."

A potion was forced into the man's mouth, although he fought savagely against it. Then his lips were held shut for several minutes. Shortly the medicine had done its work and the spy began to retch. Before their widened eyes a small silver ball flew up!

"Aha! See to that, my man," ordered Clinton. A soldier brought a tiny piece of paper from inside the ball and handed it over. It read: "Fort Montgomery Oct. 8, 1777. Here we are, and nothing between us but General Gates. I sincerely hope that this little success of ours may facilitate your operations…"

Governor Clinton immediately composed a letter to the Kingston Committee on Safety. He begged them to do all they could to defend their homes, as the British fleet was on its way. It would only have to get past West Point to proceed easily to Kingston, the most valued town before Albany. A messenger was dispatched with orders to make utmost speed.

Clinton moved his men quickly, knowing they could not arrive before the British. Five days after the first letter, Clinton sent another message. He emphasized that its contents should be given to General Gates. "Let the militia be drawn out, ready to oppose the enemy. I will be with you, if nothing extra happens, before day though my troops cannot."

Upon receiving this urgent warning, Kingston's citizens came alive with activity, burying valuables, hiding treasures in the forest, frantically filling wagons with children and women. They rushed the several miles to Hurley. On the evening of October 15, Governor Clinton saw the British fleet arrive at Kingston. The following morning he reluctantly contacted General Gates.

"I am to inform you that the evening's fleet consisting of thirty sail anchored last night about six miles below the landing place of the town..."

Within three hours the enemy had ruined the town. The few regiments from Fort Montgomery finally arrived to discover the buildings all aflame and the British on their way back to the warships.

Governor Clinton was heartbroken. "The old church—look, the courthouse—gone, more than a hundred houses lost!"

"I do see two or three houses just over there—they were not touched," one officer noted.

"Ah, yes, the Tories among them. Could we have expected anything different? It will be a bitter comfort for them to have homes when all of their neighbors have been burned!"

"At least, Sir, human life was spared. You accomplished that, with your warnings."

"Yes, thank the Lord for that little silver ball!"

Fort Stanwix

Mohawk River

N

Cherry Valley Creek

Fort Alden

ICABOD ALDEN'S
FATAL MISTAKE
Cherry Valley, 1778

It was chilly that November morning in 1778. In Cherry Valley's Fort Alden, a light snow blew around the stone corners, and the welcome smell of soup heartened the continental soldiers. Two young militiamen huddled in a stairwell, taking shelter from the wind.

"Things sure are quieter since Colonel Alden sent that scouting party out to check on any destructives coming our way."

"M-m-m. He didn't have much choice with the townspeople believing the rumors from Fort Stanwix. I thought the way they were insisting on coming to the fort we might have a real riot."

"Well, there's room enough here for them, of course, but the Colonel is convinced there's no need to worry. Can't blame the folks, though, what with all the raids nearby."

"Everyone knows that the Indians always return to their villages when it gets this late in the season, no matter what. Their tribes depend on them to hunt for their winter food. And the Tories will have to hustle to get all the way to Fort Niagara before winter."

"True. At any rate, Colonel Alden and Stacey can't be worried. They aren't even here at the fort. Guess they're staying over at the Wells place. Surely they wouldn't leave if they thought they were risking their own lives!"

"Of course not. But if they've judged wrong it will be a fatal mistake."

The men jumped at a sudden sharp crack. "What's that? Sounds like musket fire!" They scrambled up the stairs and rushed to the edge of the fort wall. The snow had turned to a cold rain. They could see a man crumpled on his horse with many people crowding around, lifting him down.

"Let's go to the gates and see what's happening!"

As they neared the entrance they were met by others who were pushing past to get away from the walls. The soldiers stopped one group.

"What is it? Who is that man?"

An older soldier answered. "Name's Hamble. Indians fired at him."

"Are they coming this way?"

"Well, Colonel Alden has assured us that there is no danger. It must be just a stray attack."

"I'm going back up—we can see more from the top," declared the younger soldier.

The two men raced to the very edge of the highest level of the fort. Others milled around restlessly, lunch forgotten. Those closest to the outer edge strained to see whatever they could. The young militiamen shivered in the rain. One turned to leave, saying "Nothing's happening. I guess it was just a scare."

"Oh, no, wait!" the other cried out. "No, no!"

His friend swung back to see what had occurred, and what he saw twisted his stomach into a knot. Scores of white troops and Indians were rushing down the pine-covered hills, dividing into groups and overrunning the town.

For a long minute none of the soldiers spoke. Each was frozen with fright. How could this be happening when Colonel Alden had been so positive there was no danger? They saw a lone figure running from the Wells house, dashing through the freezing rain. Then others followed, slipping along the muddy pathways.

"It's Colonel Alden, with Lt. Colonel Stacey!"

"He's got his pistol out—he's shooting!"

"Oh, oh, misfire!"

"An Indian over there—run, Colonel! Oh, he's been taken!"

"Don't look. It's unspeakable. Tomahawks..."

They stopped a passing officer. "We must help. What are our orders now?"

The officer slowly shook his head. "There is nothing to be done. Our senior officers are lost. We can do nothing against such carnage."

The majority of the soldiers had moved to the center of the fort for safety, but now, one by one, unable to bear the suspense, they went silently and tearfully to watch the attack. The rain was slowing to a drizzle, and house after house fell to the flames. The Indians were clearly out of control. The British apparently had abandoned the plan to take the fort itself. Occasionally, figures could be seen dashing for the protecting woods.

Late in the afternoon the devastation finally ended. The Indians had gathered many prisoners. It was a long, sad night for the Continentals, safe but feeling guilty and helpless. The only bright spot appeared when, less than forty-eight hours later, most of the captives were released. However, for the settlement of Cherry Valley, Icabod Alden's bad judgment had indeed been a fatal mistake.

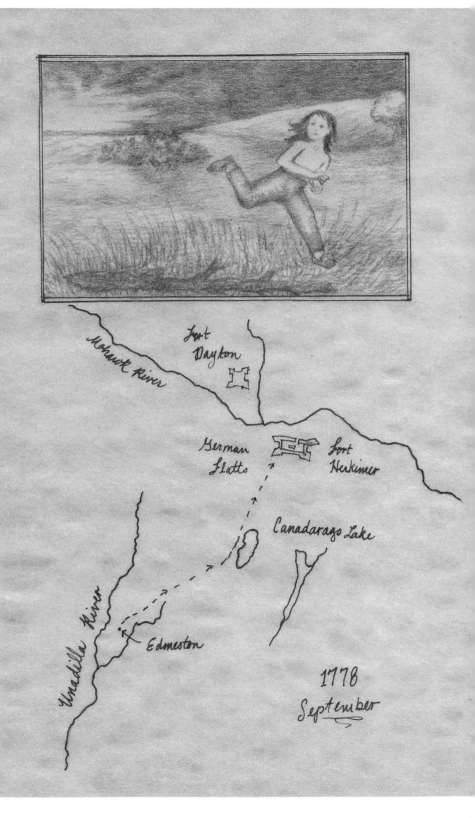

Mohawk River

Fort
Dayton

German
Flatts

Fort
Herkimer

Canadarago Lake

Unadilla River

Edmeston

1778
September

ADAM HELMER'S INCREDIBLE RUN

Edmeston, Richfield Springs,
Jordanville, Herkimer, 1778

Adam Helmer's feet were itching again! They always did when he had finished a scouting job and was back at the settlement. In 1778, German Flatts was as boring as any other section of New York. The colonists seemed too busy for anything else but building houses and working in the fields. Adam thought it was more exciting out on the trails tracking Indians than helping with the crops.

Adam yawned and stretched his arms over his head. He shook his long hair back and looked at the distant hills. He had walked every one of them. He knew each field and brook as well as he did every kitchen in the settlement. He scuffed along the path, kicking stones in the dust. A voice called out:

"Hey, Adam, watch out! I don't like to eat dirt!"

"Ho, Nate!" Adam answered, lifting a small boy off the ground. "What are you doing hiding in the bushes?"

"Scouting, just like you, Adam. Someday I can go with you, can't I?" he asked.

"Well, when you grow up..." he began.

"But I do have a message now," Nate broke in. "Colonel Bellinger wants to see you at the fort."

Adam set the boy down. "Thanks, Nate. Good thing you were around to bring the order. All the men are out haying."

"Dad says he wishes I were older. They need more hands."

Adam nodded his head. "That's right. We must get the harvest in to last us through the winter. I was going out to help. But now maybe I can go on the trail again. He hitched up his buckskins and headed for the fort.

Inside Fort Herkimer, Colonel Bellinger shook the scout's hand. "Adam Helmer!" he boomed. "Just the man for this job. We think Chief Joseph Brant is planning a raid soon."

Shivers ran up and down Adam's spine. Joseph Brant was a brave Indian warrior. Everyone had heard stories of the great chief. "You mean he's coming toward German Flatts?"

"That's what we hear. With Fort Herkimer and Fort Dayton so close together, he could try to destroy both at one time," the commander replied.

"Where is he now?"

"The last we knew, he was at Unadilla and low on supplies."

"Maybe his men will be too weak to travel."

"No, they'll restock and then most likely come this way."

"Does Chief Brant have enough Indians to take the forts?"

"Actually, we believe there are more Tories than Mohawks with him."

"Our own countrymen against us?"

"Yes. Many are still loyal to England. Brant will probably head for Percifer Carr's farm in Edmeston."

"Why there?"

"That's the closest Tory homestead. The British and Indians have brought provisions there many times."

"So I'm to see if they're meeting for a war council?"

"Yes. If so, try to find out how soon they plan to attack. We need to know if we can safely finish the harvest or if we should move our families and goods into the fort now. Choose three of the best scouts to go with you."

"Yes, sir," Adam answered. "We'll go along the Unadilla River and make camp near Edmeston. If they go near the Carr farm, we'll be waiting. We'll return the most direct way."

"Good luck! If you report danger, the cannon signal will call the colonists to the fort."

Adam and the other scouts were walking slowly as they came to the end of the trail. They'd traveled more than twenty-six miles over the high hills and stone-filled fields. The cool September air felt good on their skin, but their mouths were dry.

They were glad to find an old spring near the spot where the Indians probably would meet. The men joked as they drank the icy water, the clear liquid soothing their parched throats. Indians surely had quenched their thirst here long before any white men came. This thought gave Adam a funny feeling.

The others stretched out on the grass, but Adam was uneasy. He never could relax while working—it might cost a man his life. The strong young scout climbed up along the rock ledges. No snake ever slipped more silently over the stones! The men were out of sight now. Adam couldn't hear them talking—he wouldn't be surprised if they had fallen asleep. It had been a long trip.

Adam looked with pleasure at the quiet countryside. The land before him lay wrapped in a wispy autumn haze. Some of the maples had already begun to change color. Soon these hills would be ablaze with reds, oranges, and yellows.

Suddenly there was a flash of motion! Something alive was creeping through the bushes below! Grey shapes stepped from behind trees. Indians!

Adam crouched low and sucked in his breath. He should have stayed with the others. Had they seen the Indians yet? He couldn't call. He started to sneak back to the scouts, but froze with fear when he saw about thirty men rushing up the hill! He spun around to go higher, but several braves were sliding down the slope toward him. Trapped!

He pressed himself flat against the ground. Perspiration dampened his flesh. He heard feet near, then passing! The braves were running past him, headed to the scouts' camp. The thick bushes had hidden him. His heart beat faster when he heard shouts. That meant the others had been found. There was nothing he could do to help against so many. Three shots rang out! Then, silence.

Adam knew that he was the only scout left to carry the warning. This would only be a part of the war party. Chief Brant himself would be leading the main group, perhaps already somewhere ahead.

Adam jumped up, made his way to the edge of the cliff, and dropped over the steep ledge. There was no time to be afraid. He had scrambled through the thorn bushes and was on the trail before they saw him.

He had a good head start. They'd seen him too late, so he was out of shooting range, but a powerful runner was coming up fast! Only their best man could catch him now that he was on the trail.

Adam's heart pounded. He wanted to stop and cry for his fallen friends. But German Flatts was twenty-six miles away. If he could zig-zag to warn the families along the way, it would be even more. He had to outpace the brave so close on his heels.

Adam's rifle was holding him back, slowing him down. It was his prize possession, but it had to go. When he came to the first brook, he threw the gun into the water. He slipped off his shirt as he ran and wrapped his powder pouch and bullets in it. Then he stuffed them under some bushes. They'd be no good without the gun. Precious seconds had been lost, but they could be made up by easier traveling.

The first part of his job was done. He had the information that Brant was on the way. However, this was useless news if he couldn't get to Fort Herkimer before the enemy did. They were sure to be ahead of him, but maybe not too far. If he lost the brave chasing him, the war party wouldn't know that a warning was being brought to the fort.

Adam looked back. The runner seemed to be gaining. If he got close enough to throw his tomahawk, he wouldn't miss. It made Adam's stomach churn. The hairs on his neck prickled, but the thought of all the settlers being killed made him sprint faster. One word drummed over and over in his mind, keeping time with his feet: "Go, go, go!"

He struggled over the hills, nearly tripping several times on large tree roots and loose stones. He gathered speed as he ran along the west side of Canadarago Lake. He was tiring now and had to make himself keep pushing on.

Finally the Indian began to slow down. Adam kept his own pace steady, afraid to lose the rhythm. The distance between the two men increased. At Andrustown, Adam sensed a change. He glanced behind him, and saw that the Mohawk brave had fallen. He made no move to rise.

Adam ran on until he came to his sister Maria's house. He spoke briefly with her husband, Peter Hoyer, who gave him a change of shoes. He continued on, stopping at each house he passed, calling out the news of danger.

When there were just a few miles to go, Adam stopped to catch his breath. As he started around a bend, he saw men in the distance. He judged that there were about two hundred and knew that an equal number would be elsewhere. Certainly the forces wouldn't stand so boldly in the open if they suspected that a scout was on the way to the settlement. He had that advantage, but time was running out! The people would need quite a few minutes to get into the fort after they heard the signal.

Adam might just get to German Flatts by sunset if he ran at top speed. Brant would probably wait until dark to strike. If he was still unaware of the warning, maybe he'd wait until morning. Adam tried to forget how tired he was. His long hair hung wet against his cheeks as he ran again. His chest was very sore, each breath hurting. Thorns dug into his flesh as he pushed through brambles. He pounded across fields, praying for the strength to make the last miles.

At last, as the sun dropped behind the hills, Adam saw German Flatts ahead! Tears filled the scout's eyes. His legs trembled. But he was still running hard as he came into the settlement. People stared as he passed, hardly knowing him. He looked like a wild man, with his shirt off and his buckskin pants in tatters. His face, bare arms, and chest were covered with scrapes. Blood ran from many scratches. He called a warning to each house: "Flee for your lives! The enemy is not an hour behind!"

With his last burst of energy, Adam brought the news into Fort Herkimer. The big cannon blasted out the alarm! Across the Mohawk River, Fort Dayton heard and fired its warning signal. Every house buzzed with families gathering their goods. When the last person was safely inside, the huge gates were closed and locked. Less than one hour later, the Tories and Mohawks stood at the edge of the village.

Chief Brant was not aware that the people had been warned. A heavy rain covered up the activities around the fort. It was too miserable to set fires. The white men with Brant weren't used to long hours on the trail like his braves, so he told them to rest overnight in a nearby ravine, and the raid would begin with the first light.

Just before dawn, the warriors slipped into the settlement. The men in Fort Herkimer were alert. They were ready to fight if attacked. Women and children kept back from the outer edges of the fort. They huddled together and spoke only in whispers. When a baby cried it was quickly hushed.

While they waited, the younger boys crowded around Adam. "Why are your buckskins all ripped?" one asked.

Nate spoke up, "Don't be foolish; scouts don't stop for bushes, they go right through. That's what I'll do when I'm a scout."

"How far did you run, Adam?" one asked.

"Were there really ten Indians chasing you?" another wondered.

"No, but it felt like it. I had all I could do to outrun that one brave. Fortunately he ran out of breath first."

Suddenly one of the women grabbed Adam's arm. She began to scream and continued until Adam put his hand over her mouth. Then he saw that her house was afire! All the people crowded to the edge of the fort to see.

Now another house was in flames! Next, a large barn! Dark figures rushed among the buildings carrying lighted sticks. The flames spread, lighting the grey morning sky.

The colonists watched helplessly as their property fell into charred heaps. Torches were touched to the fields, turning them into masses of scorched grain. All of the harvest was smoldering now, both in the barns and out in the fields. Months of hard work—all lost!

Coils of black smoke smudged the sky and drifted into the fort. It stung the people's eyes and noses. Some cried when they saw their homes gone. Others shook their fists in anger. Some shouted when they saw their animals driven off into the woods. Adam tried to comfort the women and children.

At last the raid was over. Ten miles of the valley lay black and dead, chimneys standing like pokers in the rubble. Nearly one thousand animals were gone. The people were silent and sad. They knew that others outside of the settlement must have been killed. Then they realized that even though their village was ruined, they were all alive. Whispers ran through the group.

When the gates of Fort Herkimer swung open, the settlers gave a great cheer for Adam. They knew that without his warning they all would have been killed. But not one colonist from the settlement had been lost, thanks to Adam Helmer and his incredible run!

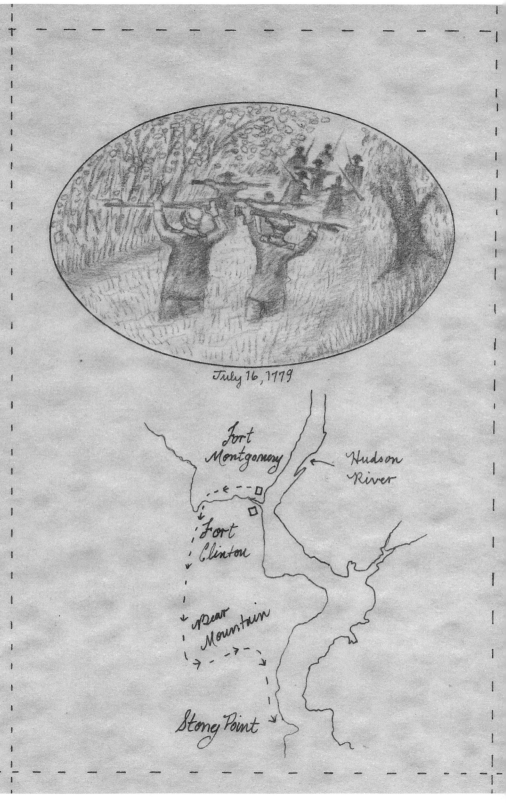

July 16, 1779

Fort Montgomery

Hudson River

Fort Clinton

Bear Mountain

Stony Point

ANTHONY WAYNE'S MIDNIGHT MARCH

Stony Point, 1779

Two generals stood on a high ridge overlooking the Hudson River. Brigadier General Anthony Wayne's face was grim as he pointed out the British-held fort to General Washington.

"You see our situation," he said. "The fort is so well guarded by both men and cannon that it would be enough to stop the best infantry, not to mention the abatis [a defensive obstacle] of pointed stakes."

"Yes, and it could hardly be more poorly located for an attack, with water on three sides and a swamp on the fourth. It would be risky indeed to try to regain the fort."

Anthony peered through his spy glass. He shook his head. "Stony Point! It's a good name for that chunk of grey rock. I'm sick to death of looking at that forsaken piece of land! I could be making a decent living back home in Philadelphia at my father's tannery."

"Don't be deceived, General; 1779 is a dismal year for all of the colonies. Few can afford to buy sugar, flour, or coffee. Why, a barrel of beef costs more than sixteen pounds! Besides, I thought you'd be anxious for revenge after that defeat at the hand of 'No Flint' Grey."

Anthony's cheeks grew red with embarrassment.

"Who ever had heard of only using bayonets in battle?"

"That could be a good strategy for our side to copy. What do you say; are you willing to try an attack?"

"Of course, Sir. I would assault Hell itself if you ordered it."

"Good. Well, I've seen enough now. Tomorrow I shall send my instructions."

Several days later, Anthony read the plan sent by General Washington.

The attack should be by the Light Infantry only, at night, with the utmost secrecy...Advance with fixed bayonets and musket unloaded...A white feather, or cockade, should be worn by our troops, and a watch-word agreed on to distinguish friends from foes.

Secrecy is more essential than numbers...If surprise takes place, the Light Infantry can do the business... Keep the knowledge of your Intention to the latest hour from all but the principal officers of your corps, and from the men, till the moment of execution.

...The usual time for exploits of this kind is a little before day...These are my ideas for a surprise, but you are at liberty to depart from them. A dark night, or even a rainy one, will contribute to your success. I am, with great regard,

Dr. Sir,
Yr. Most Obet. Servant
Go. Washington

Anthony sat for a very long time thinking about the orders and forming a more detailed plan. Then he called his leaders to his side.

He explained Washington's orders and then told his men, "It is of utmost importance that each segment of the battle plan be followed exactly. The penalty for a soldier removing his piece from his shoulder will be instant death by the nearest officer. Silence will be absolute until the moment of assault, at which time all will repeatedly shout the British troops' own victory cry as an act of rebellion.

I shall lead the right-hand column, and Colonel Richard Butler the left. Before each of these columns shall go twenty men and an officer, clearing away obstructions. Then, at the center, Major Hardy Murfree will lead two companies in creating a diversion. His will be the only troops to have loaded muskets. When the enemy is occupied with this attack, the left and right columns will rush forth to take the fort.

To make the effort more interesting there shall be awarded to the first man inside the fort a prize of $500. To the next four, sums ranging down to $100. This is our opportunity to take revenge for our last encounter with Mr. Grey!"

On July 15, the eve of the attack, Anthony dashed off a letter to a friend that he titled "Near the Hour and Scene of Carnage." He wrote that he expected to die in the battle and asked his friend to care for his children.

At midnight the brigade began its march through the thirteen-mile-long marsh. The men were from Virginia,

Pennsylvania, Connecticut, Massachusetts, Maryland, and North Carolina, thirteen hundred of these states' best. Their course was from Fort Montgomery under Torn Mountain, around Bear Mountain and along a back road.

It was extremely dark along the river road. Finally the men stopped to rest in the woods. General Wayne posted guards so no one could desert and went to look upon the fort. The British were strengthening their defenses, unaware of impending disaster. The General sent men ahead to kill every dog along their route to ensure no bark would alert the British.

The men caught Wayne's enthusiasm and were determined to win. At the narrow causeway Wayne halted his troops, then sent a few men ahead. They moved quickly, seized a sentry on watch, then bound and gagged him. In the shadows, Wayne whispered his final orders. Soldiers waded through the slimy swamp, muskets held high above the water. The sound of hundreds of men sloshing and shuffling through the muck alerted a picket who sounded the alarm. Drums boomed and British gunners sprang to their cannons! Grapeshot blasted into the darkness, but the Americans splashed ahead and the axemen went to work.

An alarm sounded from the north, and more silent, marching men appeared. They chopped away the abatis, allowing the special volunteers to race past the obstructions. Unable to return fire, the attackers clambered up the rocky slope and into the British works.

Axes continued to slash their blades into the timber. A roar of musket fire burst from the area between the two assaults, exactly as planned. The rest of the forces kept their guns silent and squeezed through the openings in the abatis. Although some fell, others stood to reach the inner ring and began to chop. The suicide squads of both columns now raced to the citadel, and the main sections silently pushed on, slowly at first, then rushing.

The repeated cries of "The fort's our own!" panicked the cornered redcoats. Quarter was called for and arms discarded. Wayne was struck by a bullet, and blood streamed down his face. The men carried him to the fort. When they came to the sally port and finally to the parapet, French Lieutenant Colonel Francois L. DeFleury was the first man over.

Wayne's wound proved to be only a scalp injury. Because so much was accomplished in only thirty minutes and in such a dramatic fashion, he earned the nickname of "Mad Anthony." News of Stony Point made a great impression on the American army and citizens alike. They had never even dreamed of a successful bayonet attack on the British. Congress voted Wayne its thanks as well as a gold medal and divided prizes from the captured stores among the troops. As promised, DeFleury and the four men behind him were afforded honors and rewards.

The British themselves acknowledged the bravery they had witnessed when Commodore Collier commented that "The rebels had made the attack with a bravery never before exhibited, and they showed a generosity and clemency which during the course of the rebellion had no parallel."

Mohawk River

Fort →

Schoharie
Creek

Fort at Middleburgh

TIMOTHY MURPHY'S BLAZING RIFLE
Middleburgh, 1780

The Schoharie Valley was peaceful that autumn day in 1780. The fort at Middleburgh sat serenely in the late afternoon sun, while colonists in the outlying cabins made their usual preparations for the coming cold season.

Within the stockade, militiaman Timothy Murphy relaxed on the wooden bench. He was glad to be off-duty for awhile, but there was little to do here. He thought back to the quiet morning in Virginia when he'd told his family that he wanted to serve the states. He'd never forgotten the responses of his loved ones.

"You're too young to go traipsin' over the country-side, young man!"

"Yes, and we could use your help right here!"

"Real fighting's not like target shooting, you know."

But Timothy had been in a fever to go. He was a good shot, and it seemed a disgrace to hang back. So he'd signed up with Morgan's rifle corps, and soon he was known as their best marksman. Then, when the Schoharie area needed men, Timothy had come to the middle fort.

He was becoming impatient, however, as there had been little action so far. There wasn't likely to be any either, as the upper and lower forts would get first crack at any invaders! He sighed and pulled out a soft cloth to polish his rifle.

Timothy was proud of his special gun. It was an unusual over-and-under, two-barreled Kentucky rifle. Once, when he was chased by a group of Indians, he shot the one running in the lead, then grabbed the dead man's gun and fired at the rest of the approaching braves. When he'd run a bit farther, he turned and shot the second time from his own rifle. This thoroughly frightened his pursuers, who couldn't understand how he could shoot twice without reloading, and they gave up the chase, believing there was something magic about him.

Timothy snapped back into the present when some-one gave a sharp whistle. He looked around, but no one was in sight. Then a freckled face peeked out from behind the corner of the building. It was Timothy's friend, Sean. He was squinting at the soldier before him and pretending to tear out his curly red hair.

"Are you polishing that rifle again? I swear you spend half your time shining that gun!"

Timothy laughed and said, "I take pride in it, that's all. It's my best friend—saved my life in the woods more than once."

"And here I thought I was your best partner! Irishmen are supposed to stick together, you know."

"Sure, and we do, don't we?" Timothy asked. Then

he lowered his voice. "We have to, with that weak-kneed commander of ours."

"Yes, Major Woolsey makes us all uneasy. I see that Colonel Vrooman is up visiting from the lower fort today. Too bad they don't change places for awhile."

"Well, we'll be all right as long as Sir John Johnson doesn't decide to show up."

"Right. The major would probably surrender at the first shot!"

"No, I don't think he'd go that far, despite the rumors about his lack of bravery. Anyway, even if the courage of the regulars should fail, there are nearly a hundred of us militiamen here. We won't shrink from action."

"I guess not!" Sean reassured his partner. "For that matter, you could probably take care of the British and the Tories yourself. As for the Indians, you know they're scared of that blazing rifle of yours!"

"Oh, come on, Sean, don't exaggerate!"

"I don't know. But then, there could be a problem. Imagine this..." A little smile began to form as Sean started in. "Johnson's men are advancing on the fort, but we're ready for them! One hundred and fifty continental troops take their positions. Now the militiamen push past them to get to the front line. But wait—one soldier is still polishing his rifle! Will he ever..."

Timothy laughed, set his rifle down, and grabbed onto Sean. "Enough of that! Unless you want to eat supper with a fat lip!"

The friends wrestled for a few minutes until they realized that the rest of the company was moving toward the dining section. They broke apart and raced each other to a table, where, once seated, they were again the dignified soldiers. It wouldn't do to get a reprimand from their superiors, so they joined the table conversation about the possibility of an attack.

Two or three of the men declared they'd welcome the chance to fight. But one young soldier wrinkled his forehead and spoke softly.

"They say Johnson has fifteen hundred men and a grasshopper."

"What are you talking about, a grasshopper?" someone asked.

"Don't you know about it? He has two mortars and a brass three-pounder. They call it a grasshopper because it is set on iron legs instead of wheels."

"That's hard to believe. How could they drag such a beast through the woods?"

"Pack horses. What else?"

The group began to look quite sober. One man added that every enemy soldier and Indian was provided with eighty rounds of cartridges.

"And here we sit with about eight rounds each!"

"What happened to our order for more?" another demanded.

"Fouled up as usual in Albany," answered an older militiaman. "But Major Woolsey sent two men out yesterday to bring us the gunpowder on their backs. They'll probably make the trip and return before the ammunition wagons!" Many laughed then, but some were nervous.

Later that night, lying sleepless on his cot, Timothy tried to imagine the steps the company actually might take if attacked. He knew the middle fort was unlikely to be tested but thought he'd feel easier if he could visualize the plan of action.

He seemed to have just fallen asleep when the call from the sentinel rang out. Timothy came fully awake at once. He couldn't believe it was really happening. He remembered that his friend, Philip Graft, was the one on duty tonight and reached for his rifle. He rushed outside to his post, surprised to see that it was already past dawn.

Graft had come down from the parapet and was pulling the sergeant of the guard over to the mud wall. The sentinel was pointing to a fire being kindled in a building at the far edge of the settlement. As he hurried away to inform the commander, three cannons boomed in the distance—the signal from the upper fort that trouble was at hand.

As the drums began to beat the alarm, Sean slipped over to Timothy. "Now they warn us! They're very good at observing the rear of an army up there. How did it get by them unnoticed?"

"At least we know they're all right at the upper fort," Timothy replied. "They can send some help if needed. Must be that Johnson didn't bother with them but just sneaked by to surprise us."

Soldiers were now tumbling from every section. When they all stood before Major Woolsey, he looked solemnly at them and then spoke, "I need volunteers to go out and discover the cause of fire. We can't tell how many of the enemy may be out there yet. It will, of course, be hazardous. Any willing men should step forward."

The words were barely out of his mouth before every man on duty moved forward, and the Major was pleased with their brave response.

"We can only spare a few," he said. "Lieutenant Spencer, you will be in charge. Count off forty men from the right and move out immediately."

Timothy was glad to be one of the forty. His hands shook a little as he prepared to leave, but he was anxious to defend his fort. Within minutes, the men were ready and started out through the gate.

The small band marched confidently toward the burning building and saw that another structure was now in flames. Did they mean to set fire to everything? Timothy knew it would be disaster for the crops to be destroyed, as the colonists depended upon their harvests to see them through the long winter.

Suddenly, the group was faced with a full company advancing upon them. Timothy felt his blood warm and rush through his veins. He'd show these fools! He raised his rifle. But after only three shots had been fired, Spencer ordered his men to go back.

The militiamen obeyed their leader reluctantly. As much as they wanted to fight, it was obvious that they had no chance to win outside of the fort. While the detachment returned with no losses except to its pride, Timothy was particularly disappointed.

"Whoever heard of going on a mission only to retreat

at the first fire?" he grumbled to Sean.

"What else could be done?" Sean asked. "You'd have all been mowed down to no purpose. At least we have a good chance now to hold them off from inside."

They watched with dismay as the coils of smoke increased. Then Sean stiffened and pointed to the east.

"Look over there! Can you believe it? They're sending in a white flag for us! I can't get over their nerve."

"Don't worry, he'll be sent packing," Timothy predicted. But, instead of giving orders to refuse this insult, Major Woolsey commanded his men to cease fire.

The officer continued to stride toward the garrison with the symbol of surrender for the fort. Timothy couldn't believe that the Major was allowing the enemy to proceed. Every soldier fell silent at the sight. They stared, shocked at the possibility of an early surrender.

Then, as the Tory came closer, Timothy rushed to the edge of the wall.

"I'll show him what we think of that color!" he shouted. He angrily raised his rifle.

One of the officers ordered him to step back. Another made a feeble attempt to restrain him. But the militia irregulars encouraged their comrade.

"Go ahead, Timothy, shoot! Let's fight to the end!"

Timothy hesitated. He knew he could easily kill the man at this range. But he decided to fire a single warning shot over the officer's head. The soldier wheeled around as the shot whistled past him, then returned at top speed to his forces.

Now the attack began in earnest! The enemy moved

forward and opened its artillery on the fort. Indians and rangers together kept up a constant musket fire. But the troops kept the guns on the ramparts furiously spurting their answer.

Timothy felt sick as he watched more houses touched by torches. A barn was now engulfed in flames. Just then, Sean came on the run.

"Timothy, come and help! We've been shelled."

Timothy inhaled sharply as he followed Sean. "I thought their shells weren't reaching us!"

"Most aren't, but the women are screaming that there's one in their quarters. And I heard another land on the roof!"

Philip Graft ran by them with a pail of water, yelling "Fire on the roof!"

Sean and Timothy reached the women's section and pushed past a group of children crowded in the doorway. "Move back—back!" Timothy ordered. The small figures stepped aside, crying.

Inside, two women were lying on their sickbeds, one moaning softly. A storm of feathers filled the room, swirling lazily before they settled.

"What the..." Sean stammered, spitting out a small feather. "Where's the..."

Timothy laughed heartily. "The shell has exploded in that feather bed over there!"

"Praise the Lord, no one was in it!" a woman said, breathing heavily. They left the women to handle the downy situation, and Sean was still coughing as they got to the roof. Philip was on his way down.

TIMOTHY MURPHY'S BLAZING RIFLE

"Too late, men!" he announced. "Took care of it myself."

The danger from within now past, the young men returned to the enemy outside the fort. As they took their places along the wall, several soldiers stepped back to get a drink.

One commented, "It's madness to try to defend this place against that many attackers!"

His partner answered soberly, "I agree. If we even had a decent supply of ammunition there might be some hope, but..."

"Well," added a third soldier, "we know what surrender would bring. If we're lucky, immediate death for us and our families. More likely it would be torture first."

The first man nodded in agreement. "The most unfortunate would be the scouts—the shirt men—especially Murphy, as he's given the enemy so much trouble." He gestured in Timothy's direction. Then he turned his head sharply. "Look! He hit one of the men behind those willows! There's another down! I swear he never misses."

The fighting continued, and to Timothy's disbelief the white flag was offered to the fort twice more during the afternoon. Each time, he sent a well-aimed warning shot close to the messenger's feet. No one bothered to reprimand him now.

"Once more, and I'm through warning!" he growled. Others were grumbling now too, as they were all tired and discouraged.

"We're perilously low on ammunition."

"Johnson doesn't know that."

"He will soon enough."

"Why didn't they send the wagons to Albany sooner?"

Then, a burst of laughter from the women's quarters drew their attention.

Timothy and several others went to investigate. They found that Major Woolsey had broken down and tried to hide with the women and children, but their laughter and ridicule had driven him out.

The story of his cowardice passed quickly from soldier to soldier. Instead of lowering their morale, the men were revived by the incident. They felt compelled to be braver than ever and fought all the harder.

But in a few minutes Major Woolsey instructed his men to gather before him. His eyes were wild with fear as he spoke.

"It grieves me to issue this order, but we can hold out no longer. We must show the white flag. See to it, Spencer. Every man lay down his arms."

Timothy exploded, shaking with anger. "What? Are you crazy? Run a white cloth up our own flagpole? Never! We promised to defend this fortress to the death. We won't meekly hand it over to those...those..."

"I'm the commander here!" Major Woolsey screamed. His fists pounded in the air over his head. "You'll follow orders like any other soldier. Obey at once!" He bobbed his head around and pointed at several officers.

One man moved toward Timothy, unsure of what to do. Timothy turned his rifle on him. "I'll shoot the first man who tries it!" he threatened in an icy tone. He stared into the eyes of the nearest men. Then cheers came from the militiamen, followed by the regulars.

"Right! We'll fight until the last of our powder is gone!" one cried. Major Woolsey stumbled away, defeated, leaving Colonel Vrooman to take command. The men returned to the battle with such intensity that Sir Johnson gave up the attack, never knowing that the colonists were nearly out of ammunition.

And so the small, brave band, inspired by Timothy Murphy, bluffed the mighty forces of Sir John Johnson.

West Point

Peekskill

Haverstraw

Hudson
River

Tarrytown

Dobbs Ferry

JOHN PAULDING'S
LUCKY FIND
West Point, 1780

Benedict Arnold was a courageous soldier and great leader of the patriot forces early in the Revolutionary War. However, his efforts were never fully appreciated and a bitterness began to grow in his heart. His desire for revenge drove him to develop a plot to surrender West Point to the British. Thus the betrayal of his country began.

Major John André, handsome young spy for the British, was sailing up the Hudson River on the H.M.S. Vulture to meet General Benedict Arnold near Haverstraw. The breeze was cool to his cheeks, yet he felt flushed, his heart beating faster as midnight approached. He mentally reviewed Sir Henry Clinton's instructions. Two tenants from the estate of Joshua Smith were to row André to shore. Just then two men approached, signaled for quiet, and helped him down the rope ladder to a waiting boat. The oars were wrapped to avoid noise, and the small craft silently moved to shore.

As André stepped onto the stony beach, three dark figures came forward. He was informed that he was speaking to General Benedict Arnold, Joshua Smith, and a servant. They left at once, hurrying to a nearby farmhouse. Here General Arnold spent several hours going over André's assignment. The General left at the break of day, allowing André to sleep at last.

The next morning André and Joshua Smith were enjoying a hearty breakfast when they heard a great noise from the river. American artillery was assaulting the Vulture, and the sloop was moving downstream. This meant they should wait until evening to begin their excursion so as to avoid suspicion.

At dusk André began his preparations. He checked the papers General Arnold had given him—a pass with Arnold's signature, which would let André through the American lines, an inventory of West Point, drawings of the complex, and plans for the British to take the fortress. He hid the folded papers in one of his boots, except for the pass which he kept in his pocket. He removed the dark blue coat and scarlet uniform he always wore and replaced them with civilian clothes. The common coat and beaver hat would be a good disguise. However, if caught without his uniform he would be considered a spy. He would take pains not to draw attention to himself.

André set out with Smith directing their paths. The horses were strong and fast, so they soon were beyond Peekskill. When Smith was about to turn back André offered to return Smith's bridle and saddle, giving his gold watch for security. Smith declined, wishing him good traveling.

It was ten o'clock on a sunny morning on Hard-scrabble Road near Tarrytown. Three scruffy appearing men lolled near a bridge playing cards. Upon hearing hoof beats, they scrambled into the bushes. André stopped as his horse nearly stepped on one of the prone bodies. At that, the three crawled out, checked shirts hanging out of their leather breeches. The apparent leader, John Paulding, proudly wore a blue coat that once adorned a German soldier who was hired by the British. His partners, Isaac Van Wart and David Williams, looked ragged beside him. While André was staring at the trio, they were eyeing his shiny leather boots, wondering how much they would fetch.

Presuming the blue coat meant these men were German, André asked, "Gentlemen, I hope you belong to our party?"

"What party might that be?" Paulding asked.

"The lower party."

"We do."

"Ah, thank God I am among friends. I am a British officer on a secret mission."

André pulled out his pass and the men tried to read it. Only Paulding could do so. "Says here this is Mr. John Anderson, on his way to Dobb's Ferry to gather intelligence for General Benedict Arnold."

Van Wart stepped back. "Maybe we should let him go; we don't want trouble."

"And maybe you don't want to eat for a few days,"

Williams replied. "Irregulars don't get the same provisions the regulars get, in case you didn't notice."

"Here, take my gold watch," André offered, "and I'll be on my way."

"No, you won't," Paulding cried, pulling André from the saddle. "See what else he has in those saddlebags and I'll check him over. Get yourself over to the bushes."

Paulding held his musket as André undressed. The others called that there was no money in the bags. "Must be in the boots—get them off."

André offered a bribe of several thousand guineas to be delivered upon his arrival at his destination.

"What guarantee would we have you'd do that?" Paulding inquired.

"You would have my word of honor."

The men hooted. "Word of honor! That's a good one. Get those boots off!"

The first boot gave up nothing, but when Paulding reached into the second he pulled out the folded papers. "Well, well, what do we have here?"

The men urged him to tell what was written, but he was concentrating on the material. At last he shared that here was an inventory of West Point, with drawings and plans for its downfall. "Looks like we should take a little trip to the outpost at North Castle. We ought to get a good reward for this!"

The Americans were surprised with the find, and the commander, Lt. Colonel Jameson, was astounded that the handwriting was the same as that on the pass—General Benedict Arnold's. He quickly sent word to

Washington, but also foolishly notified Arnold of André's arrest, thus allowing Arnold time to escape.

A week later André was tried by a jury of generals and court-martialed. Because he was captured in civilian clothes, he was denied the more dignified death by shooting and was ordered to hang as a spy. He went—dressed at last in his British uniform—and made the preparations for the gallows. He was greatly admired for the brave way he conducted himself, contrasting with the feelings Americans had for the traitor, Benedict Arnold. If it had not been for John Paulding's lucky find, West Point would have been ruined and the country's defenses severely compromised.

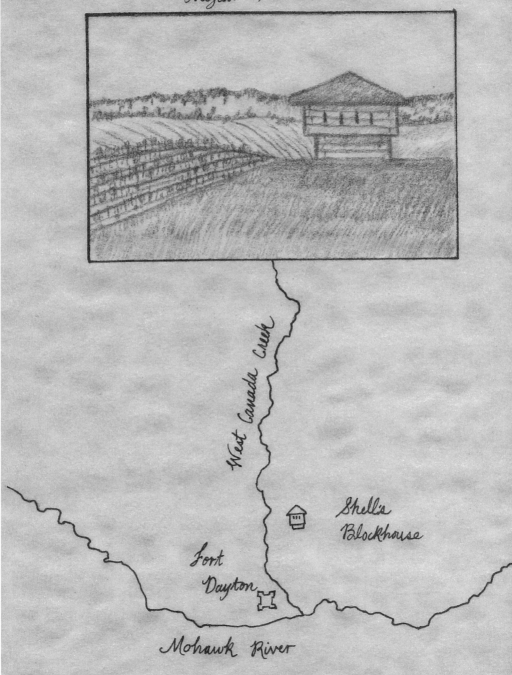

August 6, 1781

West Canada Creek

Shell's
Blockhouse

Fort
Dayton

Mohawk River

JOHN SHELL'S
TOUGH STAND
German Flatts, 1781

It was August 6, 1781. John Christian Shell had just finished eating his midday meal with his family. Shortly he would return to the fields. Although every day of harvest was precious, few farmers dared to work during this troubled period, and most of the families had taken refuge in Fort Dayton, four miles away. Donald McDonald, who headed a band of sixty-six Indian and Tories, was in the area threatening the patriots. Everyone had been advised to remain under military protection until the danger passed, but John Shell was not a man to hide.

He got up from the table reluctantly. "Mama," he said to his wife, "You're the best cook in Shell's Bush!"

"Thank you," she replied with a smile. "You know you're perfectly safe to say so. With most of the others at the fort, I may be the only cook left in Shell's Bush."

A worried look came into John's eyes. "Are you sorry you didn't go, too?" he asked.

"Of course not," Mrs. Shell replied firmly. "You've built us an absolutely secure home. Why, everyone says this blockhouse is just as safe as the stockade."

Loud scuffling noises from the corner of the room drew her attention. Two of the boys were roughhousing.

"Boys!" she commanded, "Stop that at once!" She briskly stepped across the room and grabbed the nearest son by the ear. "You two are old enough to know better. You almost knocked over my good lamp."

"Ow-w!" the young fighter protested, wriggling free. "There's nothing to do except wrestle."

"That's right, all the other guys are stuck in the fort," the disheveled victim agreed.

"Well, you won't be bored this afternoon," John told his sons. "I can use all six of you in the fields." The boys groaned, but began to get ready. The two youngest, eight-year-old twins, complained now of the heat.

"Why can't we have proper windows instead of these horrid loopholes?" one asked.

"You know very well why!" an older boy said. "It's so we can stick our guns through and shoot if we're attacked."

The other twin lifted a broomstick and pushed it into the slit. "Bang! Bang!" he yelled.

"If we did get raided, I'd go upstairs and throw things down on the enemy," another brother boasted. "The second story hangs out far enough to do it."

"That's exactly why it was built so," John informed his son. "Now come along, you rascals. We've work to do!"

He held the sturdy door open, and the six boys bounded out. The twins had a head start and were half-way across the field before John had reached the edge.

He laughed at their enthusiasm but then scoured the land for any movement in the bushes. He thought it was a disgrace that a man had to fear when on his own land. He was angry because citizens had felt forced from their homes. Well, he believed that a man's home was his castle and he refused to be driven from his!

They had been working for over an hour and were just slowing down for a short rest when a strange chill ran through John's body. Even as he stiffened, alert to danger, enemy cries cut through the afternoon air. John called to his sons, and they started towards him, frightened. But the twins were caught at the far end of the field and were quickly snatched up. John watched in horror, powerless against the large raiding party.

Then he snapped into action, roughly pushing the others ahead of him toward the house. "Run! Make for home!" he yelled.

Mrs. Shell had already flung open the door and was rushing out to the edge of the field, wild-eyed. "Is everyone safe?" she cried frantically. She counted the running figures. Three...four...

The sons pushed her back toward the house as they approached. "Go back! Get inside!" they insisted.

"The twins! Where are my babies?" she screamed.

The boys were tearful and confused as if they couldn't comprehend it all. One of them tried to go back for the younger ones. But John barred the thick door and issued orders in a voice cracking with sadness.

"No time for crying! We must save ourselves now!" His own eyes were tear-filled as he touched his wife's shoulder. "Courage, Mama," he said softly.

He handed guns to the older boys and set the younger ones in charge of the ammunition. At least there was plenty of that, he thought. His heart was hardened by the loss of his boys. He vowed not to give up another loved one, no matter how fierce the battle.

So many raiders attacked that the all the boys were soon forced to man guns alongside their father. Their mother had to do all the reloading by herself. The enemy was relentless and tried to set fire to the house again and again. But each time, the Shell family repelled the attempts.

The battle had begun at two o'clock and was still raging at dusk. Both sides were faltering. Finally, in desperation, the ferocious Donald McDonald himself slammed against the huge front door, trying to open it with a crowbar. John's musket sent a shot into McDonald's leg. Before any of his men could reach their leader, John Shell pulled open the door and yanked his prisoner in!

The boys cheered and tied up the Scotsman. The fighting had gone on for so long that their plentiful supply of lead balls and powder was nearly used up. But they took pleasure in using McDonald's supply. Soon the troops seemed to lose strength and withdrew slightly.

The family was grateful for this short rest. John was sure that as long as he held the enemy's leader his men would not burn the house. By some miracle the Shells might be able to hold out against the invaders.

The boys slumped to the floor, exhausted. Mrs. Shell

let the tears flow freely now, sitting with head bowed. She could only pray that the Tories and Indians would be merciful to her children.

John went upstairs, and soon a melody came drifting down. The boys looked at each other in surprise as they heard a familiar hymn, "A Mighty Fortress is our God." How could father sing at a time like this? But Mrs. Shell drew comfort from the words and was able to smile even as she surveyed the damaged room.

All too soon, the forces came storming back. The Shell family was revived and ready, and they met each approach with strong answering fire. Then a mighty assault was made on the house! Men rushed up close to the walls, and five of them boldly thrust the muzzles of their guns through the loopholes! Two of the slits had been occupied by the boys' weapons, which were now pushed in by the unexpected ramming. The sons were caught off balance and toppled over backwards. Shots rang out! A shocked silence came over the family.

It was a frightening situation. John directed them by gestures only so the men outside wouldn't know the positions of the household. But Mrs. Shell had finally had enough! Now she was more furious than afraid. She seized an axe and brought it down hard onto the nearest gun muzzle!

The thin barrel of the musket bent, rendering the gun useless. It was quickly withdrawn, and John immediately pushed his own musket through the slit and fired. Mrs. Shell was surprised that the weapons were so easily disabled and stepped up to the next loophole at once.

She smashed that barrel as well. While her sons watched in awe she rushed in anger to the other openings and rapidly damaged the other three guns.

As soon as each gun was removed, a boy hastened to replace it with his own. The assailants fell back in confusion. The firing lessened. Then John had an idea how to take advantage of the enemy's shock and temporary bewilderment. He ran upstairs and pretended to see the militia approaching. He called to his wife in a loud voice.

"Mama, help is here at last! Captain Small, go around the house! Captain Getman, wheel your men off to the left!"

McDonald's men, already stunned by the bent guns and weak from the long encounter, believed John's bluff. He gave such precise directions and sounded so sincere that they were convinced that the patriot troops were upon them. They fled into the woods without a backward glance.

The Shell family then hurried to the safety of Fort Dayton, leaving their prisoner in the house he had failed to capture. While they were gone, the enemy forces slipped back and went to see if McDonald was still alive. They couldn't move him because his leg was too severely injured. When they saw that the Shells had left food and water for their prisoner, the men decided to leave a message. McDonald was to tell his captors that if they continued to treat him well, his men would do the same for the Shell twins.

Captain Small saw to it that Donald McDonald was

moved to the fort the next day. His leg was amputated to save his life, but he still died within hours from loss of blood.

The young boys had been carried into Canada and were later rescued and reunited with their family. At last the courageous family was together once again in their sturdy blockhouse. John Shell's tough stand and his family's brave support had overcome tremendous odds.

BIBLIOGRAPHY

The following list is only a portion of the sources I used to discover the stories of the fifteen New York patriots featured in this book.

Alderman, Clifford Lindsey. *The War We Could Have Lost*. Four Winds, 1974.

American Heritage, Book of Historic Places. Simon and Schuster, 1957.

American Historylands. National Geographic, 1962.

Bakeless, John. *Turncoats, Traitors and Heroes*. Lippincott, 1959.

Bradford, S. Sydney. *Liberty's Road—A Guide to Revolutionary War Sites*. McGraw-Hill, 1976.

Chidsey, Donald. *The Tide Turns*. Crown, 1966.

Clarke, T. Wood. *The Bloody Mohawk*. Macmillan, 1940.

Cook, Fred J. *Dawn Over Saratoga*. Doubleday, 1973.

Cuneo, John R. *The Battles of Saratoga*. Macmillan, 1967.

Division of Archives and History. *The American Revolution in New York*. Friedman Inc., 1967.

Duprey, R. Ernest and Trevor N. *Compact History of the Revolutionary War*. Hawthorne, 1963.

Duprey, R. Ernest and Trevor, N. *An Outline of the American Revolution*. Harper, 1925.

Golden Book History of the United States, vol. 3. Golden Press, 1969.

Great Epochs in American History. Current Lit. Publishing Col, 1916.

Hagan, Edward A. *War in Schohary 1777–1783*. Self-published, 1980.

Halsey, Francis W. *The Old New York Frontier*. Scribner's, 1913.

Hamilton, Edward P. *Fort Ticonderoga*. Little Brown, 1964.

Hislop, Codman. *The Mohawk*. Rinehart, 1948.

Lancaster, Bruce. *American Heritage Book of the Revolution*. American Heritage / Simon & Schuster, 1958.

Langguth, A.J. *Patriots—The Men Who Started the American Revolution*. Simon & Schuster, 1988.

Lomask, Robert. *The First American Revolution*. Farrar, Straus and Giroux, 1974.

Leckie, Robert. *Great American Battles*. Random House, 1968.

Leckie, Robert. *The Wars of America*. Harper, 1981.

Marshall, Douglas W. and Peckham, Howard. *Campaigns of the American Revolution*. U. of Michigan and Hammond, 1976.

McDowell, Bart. *The Revolutionary War*. National Geographic, 1967.

Meltzer, Milton. *The American Revolutionaries—A History in Their Own Words 1750–1800*. Thomas Y. Crowell, 1987.

Sobol, Donald. *American Revolutionary War Reader*. F. Watts, 1964.

Stone, William A. *A Life of Brant, vol. III*. Alexander Blade, 1838.

Symonds, Craig. *Battlefield Atlas of the American Revolution*. Nautical and Aviation Publishing Co., 1986.

Van Every, Dale. *A Company of Heroes*. Morrow, 1962.

Vrooman, John J. *Council Fire and Canon*. Follett Publishing Co., 1962.

Vrooman, John J. *Forts and Firesides of the Mohawk Country*. Baronet Litho Co., 1951.

Wheeler, Mary A. *New York State, Yesterday and Today*. Scribner, 1952.

Whitney, David. *Colonial Spirit of '76 People of the Revolution*. Encyclopedia Britannica, 1974.

Wood, W.J. *Battles of the Revolutionary War*. Duell, Sloan and Pearce.

ABOUT THE AUTHOR

Dorothy Loyte Blackman grew up in Jamaica Plain, Massachusetts, graduated from Lynn English High School in Lynn, Massachusetts, and attended Gordon College in Boston. She was a substitute teacher for several New York schools on all grade levels for thirty-one years. She has been the Library Manager of the Edmeston Free Library for twenty-five years. Her husband, the Reverend John A. Blackman, Pastor Emeritus, served the First Baptist Church in Oswegatchie, New York, and the Second Baptist Church in Edmeston, New York. Dorothy has been a minister's wife for fifty fulfilling years.

"Dottie" and her husband still live in Edmeston. They have four adult children and seven grandchildren. Besides having greeting cards and short stories published, her writing credits include *Seventeen Magazine* and *Mohawk Valley USA*, a regional magazine which originally published several of these stories.